IT'S TIME FOR WINE

A BEGINNER'S GUIDE TO WINE TASTING

ELLEN BLAIR

CONTENTS

INTRODUCTION

If you like a good glass of wine, you're not alone. But what does a good glass of wine actually taste like? Well, this book is going to help you answer that question so that you can start tasting wine just like the pros! Wine has been around for a long time, and cultures have been perfecting the various recipes throughout history. The earliest evidence of wine is found in what is now the Eurasian state of Georgia, and it is dated circa 6000 BC. Since those early days, wine has come to symbolize many different things to different cultures. Ancient Egyptians associated red wine with blood, and both red and white wine has been used by cultures as varied as the ancient Greeks and Israelis for sacred religious rituals.

While wine has played a significant role in history, in the modern world, there's nothing like a good glass of wine to top off a savory dinner or relax after a hard day's work. But, exactly what does a good glass of wine taste like? You've probably heard the descriptions, "It has an oaky finish," or, "It's an earthy wine." What exactly do those mean, and what does earthy taste like? Those are the kinds of questions this book aims to answer.

This book will be your go-to guide for everything wine. I'll introduce you to the grape and the journey it makes to get to your wine glass. You'll learn about the best grapes for making the best wine, the different types of wine, the difference between Old World and New World wines, how to improve your wine palate, wine tasting etiquette, and much more. With the information you learn in this book, you'll be able to go out and swirl wine with the best of them. You'll know what to look for in a truly great-tasting wine, and you'll understand the technique for proper wine sampling. And, what's more, you'll discover the numerous and significant health benefits of wine. That's right, wine is actually good for you, and there's scientific evidence to back that up.

It's no wonder that wine has been described as a necessary prerequisite for the development of civilization itself. It definitely makes me more civil after a hard day of work. In fact, Socrates himself said, "We are brought by the gentle persuasion of wine to a happier mood." And, Euripides – a Greek playwright and poet – wrote, "Where there is no wine, love perishes, and everything else that is pleasant to man." While you probably wouldn't recognize those ancient elixirs as wine, much of the same sentiment holds true for wine today. Some 240 million people in the US alone are wine drinkers for many of these same reasons.

So, if you're one of the millions who enjoy wine, but don't know as much as you'd like to know about it, this book will change that. If you'd like to know more about how to pick a great tasting wine, one that fits the occasion as well as the meal, then read on. With this book, you'll go from feeling like a complete novice to impressing your friends and family with your wine tasting acumen. You will be confident in your knowledge of wine and your skills of wine tasting to the degree that you'll never again doubt your ability to pick an excellent wine for any situation, and your friends and family will turn to you as the expert on the subject.

The methods of wine tasting presented in this book will help you to easily understand what exactly is meant by a good glass of wine. There's no reason to wait another day or spend another dime on choosing the wrong wine that's poor quality. This book will be an invaluable resource you'll turn to again and again as you increase your skill in wine tasting. And, it will be worth its weight in gold when it saves you from spending good money on bad wine. With this book, you can pick a great wine for tonight's dinner. It will bring you immediate value, and as a true wine lover, you won't want to miss out on all the benefits you'll get from the knowledge in the following chapters. So, best get cracking, because it's time for wine!

CHAPTER ONE: THE JOURNEY OF THE GRAPE

As you sit sipping on that delicious and relaxing glass of wine, you might be wondering just how the grape arrived in your glass as this enticing elixir. Well, sit back, pour a second glass, and let me take you on a journey from grape to wine glass. Let's start with the basics.

GRAPEVINE BASICS

A grapevine is a perennial plant; that means it grows and blooms in the spring and summer, dies back during the fall and winter, and then repeats the cycle the following spring. If no humans ever intervened in that cycle, the vine would grow into a bushy-like tree of tangled leaves and branches. Only with meticulous pruning will the vines stay organized. Keeping them organized allows the plant to focus more energy on growing tasty grapes.

While there are some sixty different species of grapevines, most of the quality wine in the world comes from one type: *Vitis vinifera*. When the vine is planted, the first year of life is used for building up a store of valuable nutrients, much like a growing child needs to eat their vegetables to grow strong. During this stage, any flower clusters that develop are typically pruned. That lets the vine focus its energy on establishing a strong root system. You've got to have a good foundation to produce quality wine, and the root system is that foundation.

By the time the vine is in its third year of growth, it's ready to produce good quality fruit for winemaking. The vine will mature over the course of 30 years, so there will still be plenty of good grape-producing years left by this point.

Winter Pruning

Aside from harvesting the grapes, one of the most important activities is winter pruning. During this time, the pruner will select the best canes to grow new shoots from for the coming year's harvest. The goal is to achieve a maximum yield of good quality grapes.

Winter pruning is carried out when the vines are

dormant, and it is used to maintain the vine training system. Grapes are only produced on shoots that are growing from one-year-old canes. The new canes grow from the head of the vine, which is referred to as the canopy. So, to get fruit every year, healthy new canes need to be selected and retained. Unnecessary canes are pruned. This "trains" the vines to grow in a way that is conducive to harvesting, and it also shapes the location and development of the canopy. If you have too many buds, that can result in a crowded canopy where there will be too much shade. Additionally, the vine may not be capable of ripening all of the fruits if there are too many.

This means the goal of the pruner is to create a well-constructed canopy that will produce just enough high-quality grapes – it's the Goldilocks equation, you don't want too many or too few. You want just the right amount. If the vine is well-trained, that will produce a good overall grape yield, and a healthy, well-developed vine. So, each winter, the vines are pruned in anticipation of the next year's harvest, and with the shaping of the canopy in mind.

Springtime in Wine Country

In April/May in the northern hemisphere or September/October in the southern hemisphere, sap begins to rise up from the roots and buds form on the canes. At this point, the buds are very delicate and at high risk of being destroyed by natural forces like hailstorms. In fact, some vineyards have lost 100% of their buds from hail.

After the buds form, or break as it is referred to, the viti-culturalists – fancy word for winegrower – will prune the downward-facing shoots so that all shoots are growing upward. This also reduces the potential yield, but by reducing quantity, you increase quality since the more limited number of grapes means more concentrated flavor.

Summer Flowers

By June and July (Nov/Dec in the southern hemisphere), young flower clusters will appear. The flowers of a grapevine are known as perfect flowers since they are able to pollinate themselves without needing bees. These flower clusters will become berry bunches. The berries are green to begin with, but by mid to late summer, they start to change color as they ripen. This is called vérasion (verre-ray-shun), and it's the most colorful time of the year in the vineyard. The berries change from green to yellow, pink, red, or purple.

Right before vérasion, many winegrowers will perform what is called green harvesting whereby they remove the superficial grape bunches, which reduces the weight from the vine. That, again, allows the vine to focus on ripening fewer grapes, but with higher quality. While the grapes are ripening, and sugar levels are rising, the wood of the vine continues to grow and ripen over the summertime. As it does, it will turn brown and harden, something called lignifying.

Harvest

Harvesting the grapes usually occurs between September and November – or February and May in the southern hemisphere – when the grapes are in what wine growers refer to as the "sweet spot." The goal is to harvest the grapes when they have reached their perfect ripeness. Since grapes do not continue to ripen once they're picked, harvesters work around the clock when the grapes are ripe. Some growers will leave a few grape bunches on the vine for a late-harvest wine. Those grapes dry out – or raisinate – and are then pressed which produces a very sweet dessert wine.

Back to Sleep

By late in the fall, the vine is no longer producing carbo-hydrates from the chlorophyll in the leaves, and the leaves will then lose their color and fall to the ground. From November to May, as winter returns, the foliage on the vine dies, and it's time again for winter pruning. But, of course, this is only part of the story. Now, we have grapes, but we want wine.

From Grape to Great – Stomp!

A grape that is ripened to perfection is full of natural sugars, and it also has wild yeasts living on its skin. What the winemaker wants to do is gently crush the grapes to release the sugary juice inside and expose it to the yeasts on the skin. Throughout the ages, three methods of crushing the grape have dominated around the world; these vary from bare feet to elaborate, computer-controlled devices. But first, it's important to understand there is a difference between crushing and pressing grapes. Crushing simply breaks the grape berries, thereby exposing the juices to the skin yeasts, while pressing involves separating the grape juice from the fiber and other solid materials that make up the grape. Crushing and pressing can be done at the same time, or they can be separated by a few hours or days. The time between crushing and pressing depends on the style of wine that's being made.

The first step in processing the grape is to decide if it will be crushed "whole cluster". That means will it be crushed with the stem intact? Stems add extra tannin and structure to developing wines, which is great for red and orange wines, but for white wines and some light reds, the extra tannins are undesirable, and therefore, the winemaker will separate the stems from the berries before crushing. Once that decision is made, it's time for the crush.

The oldest method of whole-cluster crushing is to stomp on it with your feet. It's called foot treading, and it's most popular today in Portugal. This is accomplished using three or four workers who first wash their feet in bacteria-killing sulfur solutions before getting into the crushing bins or stone lagares. It will typically take them several hours to crush the grapes, and traditionally, they do this performing a dance that comes with sides of brandy and roasted chestnuts – might as well make it a fun process. While grapes may appear delicate, grapes are denser than they seem and require several hours of stomping to thoroughly mix the grape juice and solids.

A more popular, faster method of both crushing and destemming grapes involves metal machines that separate the stems from the berries, and then, gently break open their skins. The wineries that do this typically dump the grapes from a truck bed into large metal hoppers that funnel the grapes into the destemmer. That rotates to remove the stems while at the same time letting the berries fall into another machine where they are lightly crushed. From there, the grapes will either be moved to tanks to begin the fermentation process with their skins, or they will be moved into a press.

Sometimes, the wine press also doubles as a crusher. In that case, the grapes don't spend any time marinating with the skins before beginning the fermentation process. That is usually the process in the production of the most delicate white wines where the juice runs straight away from the pulp and seeds, thereby retaining its pure, varietal characteristics. In the modern age, most wineries will use a pneumatic press for crushing grapes. These have a large, plastic balloon that will gradually inflate to very gently break the grape skin. The juice then drains into a pan beneath the press, which rotates to get every drop. After several hours, the press turns and inflates again, and the process is repeated. The winemaker is left with a pile of dry skins and seeds by the end of this process.

Fermentation

After the grapes have been foot-treaded, machine crushed, or pressed as the case may be, now it's time to make use of that chemistry class material you never thought you'd have a chance to use. In the lab, winemakers monitor and test the fermentation process. Fermentation requires sugars and yeasts. The sugars are in the juices of the grape and the yeasts are one the skin. So, theoretically, all that is needed is to mix the two and wait. When the resulting alcohol reaches approximately 15 percent, the yeasts die naturally, and any sugar left over will remain in the wine. But, of course, the devil's in the details.

Yeasts: Natural wines are fermented only with the wild yeasts found on its skin, and those are native to its territory.

Yeast strains vary from location to location, and they make a significant contribution particularly to the odor of the finished wine. In fact, yeasts are a vital part of what gives wine its character. Many winemakers will kill the natural yeasts on the skin of the grape and add a single strain of commercially produced yeast. This results in less personality in the wine, and makes it less complex in its flavor. That's why so many wines from different regions taste the same – they've been fermented with the same yeast.

Sugars: Sugars determine the level of alcohol in the finished wine. More sugar means more for the yeast to convert into alcohol. Grapes grown further north have less sun, and that translates into less stored sugar than grapes grown in the south. Therefore, traditionally, wines produced in the north contain a lower level of alcohol. But, winemakers have another tool in their kit. Chaptalization is a way to boost the level of alcohol by adding sugar to the juice during the fermentation process. The technique is named after the Agriculture Minister in Napoleon's administration who is said to have invented it – Jean Antoine Chaptal. Natural wines, however, are fermented only with their own sugars.

Malolactic Fermentation: This refers to a secondary process involving bacterial conversion. This can follow or overlap with the primary fermentation process. Malic acid is a harsher tasting chemical that is converted into the less acidic lactic acid. During the process of conversion, carbon dioxide is also produced. This conversion process results in a reduction in the acidity of the wine and an increase in its complexity. The level of alcohol, however, remains the same. This process can be induced by introducing cultured bacteria or by suppressing sulphur dioxide – or SO^2 – which inhibits the process. Wines that are bottled quickly will often have SO^2 added to the bottle to prevent the malolactic fermentation inside the bottle. Natural wines are those where this process occurs naturally, and the winemaker must wait for it to finish before bottling.

Wine and Culture

With such an intricate production process, it's no wonder that wine has been a major part of many cultures throughout history. In 1779, for example, Benjamin Franklin mused that the location of the elbow is proof that "God desires us to drink wine." He noted that had the elbow been located lower on the arm, the glass would not make it to our mouths. He went on to say, "Let us adore and drink!" While he was most certainly being facetious, his words are but one example of the prominent role of wine in many cultures and rituals. In fact, wine and religion are long-time companions.

Among the Egyptians, wine was associated with several of their gods, such as Hathor, who was considered the patron god of wine. As early as 4,000 BC, he was honored with a monthly, "Day of Intoxication." The Greeks considered the god Dionysus as the giver of all good gifts, and among those gifts was wine since he was also the patron god of wine. The Romans, on the other hand, believed that wine was given to the human race by Jupiter, the god of air, light, and heat. Roman festivals all coincided with the various phases of grape-growing and wine-producing.

Asian cultures also associated wine with the spiritual aspect of life. Japanese Shinto shrines include large casks of sake, and wine is placed on ceremonial altars to honor the Chinese god of prosperity. Judaism and Christianity also consider wine a sacred elixir. In Hebrew scriptures (Genesis 27:28, Deuteronomy 7:13) wine is described as a sign of God's blessing, and in the Christian New Testament, the first public miracle performed by Jesus was turning water into wine at the wedding at Cana. Furthermore, the Christian sacrament of Communion whereby priests supply sacramental wine to worshipers is another way that religion has used wine as part of a sacred ritual.

When the first American colonists came to the New World, they quickly began making wine which was used to celebrate the first Thanksgiving in 1623. By 1697, Jesuit priests in Baja, California immediately planted grapes upon arriving in the area so they would be able to supply the mission with a reliable source of wine for Communion and for drinking with their meager meals. This mission, along with several others built in various locations in California helped make the future state the wine-producing nucleus of the United States. As more colonists settled throughout North America, they too used wine to promote a sense of camaraderie that helped them bond as Christian communities. In fact, many Protestant congregations reported that wine produced an altered mood in congregants that was conducive to religious fervor.

Wine was not seen as the nectar of the gods by all, however, as temperance advocates pushed for the prohibition of alcohol. There were many reasons for the Volstead Act which enforced Prohibition between 1920 and 1923 in the United States, but lawmakers were loath to include wine. They ensured that the production of "Medicine of Life to the Nations" (that's wine) was protected for both Christian and Jewish congregations. But, not all ministers thought of wine as necessary for their rituals. One notable example is Thomas Welch, a Methodist minister who became a dentist. He was strident in his opposition to alcohol, and so, he set about perfecting a fermentation process that removed the alcohol-producing yeast from the grape juice. He then founded the Welch Company in 1869 that substituted Welch's grape juice for the purpose of Communion. Welch considered he was providing his church with the "fruit of the vine," instead of the "cup of devils." Benjamin Franklin would surely have disagreed with Welch's view as exemplified by his reference to wine as, "Proof that God loves us, and loves to see us happy."

It's sentiments such as that which led to the United States being one of the major wine-producing nations in the world today. The US, along with Italy, France, and Spain, are the biggest wine-producing nations. Spain has the largest vineyard, and surprisingly, China is in second place. Still, the US holds the record as the biggest wine consuming nation, followed by France, Italy, and Germany. Chile, however, has seen the most growth in wine production in the past five years. And, they are all producing some tasty types of wine, as you may already know. The following is a list of wine varieties, from A to Z with a description of their flavor. Find your favorites from the list below and see if you agree with the description!

- **Albariño**

This Spanish white wine is made from a grape that makes crisp, refreshing, and light-bodied wines.

- **Aligoté**

This white wine grape is grown in Burgundy, and it makes medium-bodied, crisp, dry wines with spicy character.

- **Amarone**

This wine is from Italy's Veneto Region, and it is a strong, dry, long-lived red wine, made from a blend of partially dried red grapes.

- **Arneis**

This is a light-bodied dry wine from the Piedmont Region of Italy.

- **Asti Spumante**

From the Piedmont Region of Italy, this is a semi-dry sparkling wine from the Moscato di Canelli grape in the village of Asti.

- **Auslese**

This is a German white wine produced from grapes that are very ripe, and thus, high in sugar.

- **Banyuls**

This is a French wine made from late-harvest Grenache grapes and served with chocolate or dishes with a hint of sweetness. By law, this wine must contain 15 percent alcohol.

- **Barbaresco**

A red wine from the Piedmont Region of Italy, made from Nebbiolo grapes. This wine is lighter than Barolo (see below).

- **Bardolino**

This is a light red wine from the Veneto Region of Italy. It is blended from several grapes that produce a wine garnet in color, dry, and slightly bitter, though also sometimes lightly sparkling.

- **Barolo**

This is a highly regarded Italian red, made from Nebbiolo grapes. It is dark, full-bodied, and high in tannin and alcohol. It is a wine that ages well.

- **Beaujolais**

These are typically light, fresh, fruity red wines from an area south of Burgundy, near Lyons, in eastern France. The regions that produce these wines include the following: Beaujolais-Blanc, Beaujolais Villages, Brouilly, Chénas, Chiroubles, Fleurie, Juliénas, Moulin-à Vent, Morgon, Regnie, Saint Amour.

- **Blanc de Blancs**

This is a champagne or white wine made from white grapes.

- **Blanc de Noirs**

This is a white or blush wine or champagne made from dark grapes.

- **Blush**

This is the American term for rosé, which refers to any wine that is pink in color.

- **Boal or Bual**

This is made from grapes grown on the island of Madeira, which produce medium-sweet wines.

- **Brunello**

This strain of Sangiovese is the only grape allowed to be used for Brunello di Montalcino, the rare, costly Tuscan red. The flavor consists of luscious black and red fruits with chewy tannins.

- **Cabernet Franc**

This is a red wine grape used in Bordeaux for blending with Cabernet Sauvignon. It's lower tannin levels make it an earlier maturing red wine. It is a light- to medium-bodied wine with more immediate fruit than Cabernet Sauvignon. Additionally, it has some of the herbaceous odors evident in unripe Cabernet Sauvignon.

- **Cabernet Sauvignon**

The Cabernet Sauvignon flavors include Currant, Plum, Black Cherry & Spice, with notes of Olive, Vanilla Mint, Tobacco, Toasty Cedar, Anise, Pepper & Herbs. These are full-bodied wines with great depth that improve with aging. Cabernet spends from 15 to 30 months aging in American & French oak barrels which tend to soften the tannins, adding the toasty cedar & vanilla flavors.

- **Carignan**

This is known as Carignane in California, and Cirnano in Italy. Once a major blending grape for jug wines, Carignan's popularity has diminished though it still appears in some blends. Carignan wine from old vineyards is sought after for the intensity of the grapes.

- **Carmenere**

This is also known as Grande Vidure and was once widely planted in Bordeaux. Now it is primarily associated with Chile after having been imported to Chile in the 1850s. Carmenere has been frequently mislabeled by many growers, and the Chilean government considers it a Merlot.

- **Cava**

This is a Spanish sparkling wine, produced by the méthode champenoise.

- **Charbono**

This wine is mainly found in California (may possibly be Dolcetto), though this grape has dwindled in acreage. It is often lean and tannic, which is why few wineries still produce it.

- **Champagne**

Champagne is the only wine that people accept in such a multitude of styles. Champagnes can range from burnt, caramelly oxidized to full-bodied fruit and yeast characters, and from there, to light and citrusy, and everything in between. Moreover, each of these wines can be altered in the amount of residual sweetness, from a bone-chilling dryness to sugary syrup. The bottle age will also alter the weight and character of each of these styles.

- **Chardonnay**

The flavors for Chardonnay include Apple, Pear, Vanilla,

Fig, Peach, Pineapple, Melon, Citrus, Lemon, Grapefruit, Honey, Spice, Butterscotch, Butter, and Hazelnut. Chardonnay takes well to oak aging and barrel fermentation, and is easy to manipulate with techniques such as sur lie aging and malolactic fermentation.

- **Châteauneuf-du-Pape**

This refers to the most famous wines of the southern Rhône Valley, which are produced in and around the town of the same name (the summer residence of the popes during their exile to Avignon). The reds are rich, ripe, and heady, with full alcohol levels and chewy rustic flavors. Although 13 grape varieties are planted here, the primary varietal is Grenache, followed by Syrah, Cinsault and Mourvèdre (also Vaccarese, Counoise, Terret noir, Muscardin, Clairette, Piquepoul, Picardan, Roussanne, Bourboulenc).

- **Chenin Blanc**

This is the native wine of the Loire where it's the basis of several famous whites: Vouvray, Anjou, Quarts de Chaume and Saumer. In other areas it is a very good blending grape. Called Steen in South Africa, it is their most frequently planted grape. California uses it mainly as a blending grape for generic table wines. It can be a pleasant wine, with melon, peach, spice, and citrus flavors. The great Loire wines, depending on the producer, can be anywhere from dry and fresh to sweet.

- **Chianti**

Produced from a blend of grapes, this fruity, light ruby-to-garnet-colored red may be called Chianti Riserva when aged three or more years.

• Chianti Classico

This is produced in a specifically designated portion of the Chianti wine district in Italy. To be labeled Chianti Classico, both vineyard and winery must be within the specified region.

• Claret

British term for red Bordeaux wines.

• Colombard (French Colombard)

This is the second most widely planted white variety in California, and nearly all of it is used for jug wines. It produces an abundant crop – nearly 11 tons per acre – and makes clean, simple wines.

• Constantia

This legendary sweet wine from South Africa was a favorite of Napoleon. It comes from an estate called Groot Constantia.

• Cortese

This white wine grape is grown in Piedmont and Lombardy in Italy. It's best known for the wine known as Gavi. The grape produces a light-bodied, crisp, well-balanced flavor.

- **Dolcetto**

This wine is from the northwest Piedmont region in Italy, and it produces soft, round, fruity wines fragrant with licorice and almonds.

- **Eiswein**

The term means "Ice wine," and is a sweet German wine, made from grapes that have frozen on the vine. Freezing concentrates the sugars in the grapes before they are harvested.

- **Frascati**

This is an Italian fruity, golden white wine that varies from dry to sweet.

- **Fumé Blanc**

See Sauvignon Blanc

- **Gamay**

Beaujolais, known for its famous, fruity reds, makes them exclusively from one of the many Gamays available, the Gamay Noir à Jus Blanc. Low in alcohol and relatively high in acidity, the wines are meant to be drunk soon after bottling; the ultimate example of this is Beaujolais Nouveau, which is rapidly dispersed onto store shelves everywhere almost overnight.

- **Gamay Beaujolais**

A California variety that makes undistinguished wines, and is primarily used for blending.

- **Gattinara**

A Piedmont red made from Nebbiolo and blended with other grapes, this wine has a powerful and long-lived flavor.

- **Gewürztraminer**

This is a medium-sweet wine with a distinctive floral bouquet and spicy flavor. It's grown mainly in the Alsace region of France and Germany, but it is also grown in California, Eastern Europe, Australia, and New Zealand.

- **Grappa**

This is an Italian spirit distilled from pomace. It is dry and high in alcohol, and it is considered an after-dinner drink.

- **Grenache**

This is used mainly for blending and the making of Rose and Blush Wines in California, and in France, it is blended to make Chateauneuf-du-Pape. It is originally from Spain, and it is the second most widely grown grape in the world. It yields a fruity, spicy, medium-bodied wine.

- **Johannisberg Riesling**

See Riesling.

- **Kir**

This is an aperitif from the Burgundy region of France. It is made with a glass of dry white wine and a teaspoon of crème de cassis. It is also one of the more popular drinks. To make Kir Royale, use champagne or sparkling wine instead of a regular white wine.

• Lambrusco

This is a fizzy, dry to sweet Italian wine that is usually a red. It is made from the grape of the same name.

• Liebfraumilch

This is a blended German white, semisweet and fairly neutral. It accounts for up to 50 percent of all German wine exports.

• Madeira

This is a fortified wine that is named for the island where the grapes are grown. Styles include dry aperitifs made from the Sercial grape as well as rich and sweet Boal and Malmsey varieties.

• Malbec

This is an important wine for blends in Bordeaux and Loire in the past, but it has been replaced by Merlot and the two Cabernets. Argentina, however, is now using this successfully. In the US, it's only used for blending, and it's not very significant mainly because it's considered part of the Bordeaux blend recipe.

• Marc

This is distilled from pomace, and in Italy, it's called grappa, in Burgundy, Marc de Bourgogne, and in Champagne, Marc de Champagne. It is high in alcohol content, and typically used as a dry, after-dinner drink.

- **Marsala**

This is made from Grillo, Catarratto, or Inzolia grapes in Sicily where the wine is dry or sweet and frequently used for cooking.

- **Marsanne**

This is a full-bodied, moderately intense wine with spice, pear and citrus flavors. It is popular in Rhone and Australia, where there are some of the world's oldest vineyards. A California winery, Rhone-Rangers, has also had considerable success with this variety.

- **Mead**

Mead was common in medieval Europe, and it is made by fermenting honey and water. Today, many winemakers make flavored meads.

- **Meritage**

This blends two or more Bordeaux grape varieties, and it was registered in the United States in 1989. It's a new name because the wines produced don't use 75 percent of a single grape variety. The name is a combination of merit and heritage, and to carry this label, the wine must be the result of the Bordeaux grape blends and have less than 90 percent of any single variety. Additionally, it has to be the best wine of its type and be produced and bottled in a US winery from grapes carrying a US appellation. It is also limited to a maximum of 25,000 cases produced per vintage.

- **Merlot**

This variety takes well to oak aging, and it is a softer, medium-weight wine with fewer tannins than Cabernet. It's also ready to drink sooner and is frequently used for blending with Cabernet to soften the flavor.

- **Montepulciano**

This is a medium to full-bodied wine, with good color and structure. It's well-known for its quality and value.

- **Moscato**

See Muscat.

- **Mourvedre**

This is a pleasing wine, of medium-weight, with spicy cherry and berry flavors and moderate tannins. It is frequently used in Châteauneuf-du-Pape.

- **Müller-Thurgau**

This is a cross between two grapes: Sylvaner and Riesling. It's mainly grown in Germany, northern Italy, and New Zealand, and it's light in color and dry to medium-dry.

- **Muscat**

This is also called Muscat Blanc and Muscat de Canelli, and it has pronounced spice and floral notes that also make it great for blending. It is a versatile grape that can be used in anything from Asti Spumante and Muscat de Canelli to the dry Muscat d'Alsace.

- **Nebbiolo**

This is the great grape of Northern Italy. It produces excellent, strong, agreeable wines in Barolo and Barbaresco. Nebbiolo is also now produced to a lesser degree in California. The wines there, however, are light and uncomplicated, bearing no resemblance to the Italian styles.

- **Petit Verdot**

This wine is from the Bordeaux region in France, and it is used mainly for blending with Cabernet Sauvignon.

- **Petite Sirah**

This wine has a deep, ruby color and plum and black-berry flavors. It is full-bodied with chewy tannins, and it is used in France and California as a blending wine. It is not related to the Syrah of France.

- **Pinot Blanc**

This wine is similar in texture and flavor to Chardonnay. It can be intense and complex with notes of ripe pear, citrus, spice, and honey. It is produced in Champagne, Burgundy, Alsace, Germany, Italy, and California.

- **Pinot Grigio/Pinot Gris**

At its best, these wines are soft, perfumed, and more colorful than other white wines. This is grown mostly in northeast Italy, but Pinot Gris is also grown in Alsace and Tokay.

- **Pinot Meunier**

This grape is grown in the Champagne region in France, and it is blended with Pinot Noir and Chardonnay for adding fruit flavors to champagne.

- **Pinot Noir**

This is a noble grape of Burgundy, but it's a difficult one to grow. It produces a smooth, rich Cabernet Sauvignon with fewer tannins. It has raisin-like flavors and undertones of black cherry, raspberry, and spice. It is used frequently for making champagne sparkling wines.

- **Pinotage**

This is a cross between Cinsault and Pinot Noir that is grown in South Africa. It is fermented at higher temperatures and aged in new oak, which produces marvelous berry flavors.

- **Port**

This is a fortified wine produced in the Douro region of Portugal. The styles for this include Late Bottle, Tawny, Ruby, Aged, and Vintage, and all are mostly sweet and red.

- **Retsina**

This is a dry, white Greek wine that is flavored with pine resin. It is an acquired – the dominant flavor is turpentine, but it also has Riesling flavors that include apricot and tropical fruit with floral aromas. The styles of this ancient Greek wine vary from dry to sweet.

- **Rosé**

This is sometimes called blush, and it refers to any light pink wine that is dry to sweet and made by removing the skins of red grapes early in the fermentation process. It can also be made by mixing red and white varieties.

- **Roussanne**

This is a white wine grape of the northern Rhône Valley, and it is mainly used for blending with the Marsanne white wine grape.

- **Sangiovese**

This wine is known for its supple texture and medium to full-bodied spice flavors with raspberry, cherry, and anise. It is used in the production of many fine Italian wines, such as Chianti.

- **Sauternes**

This is a blend of Sauvignon and Semillon grapes. It is affected by *Botrytis cinerea*, which concentrates the wine's alcohol and sweetness.

- **Sauvignon Blanc**

This wine is known for its grassy and herbaceous flavors and aromas. It is a light and medium-bodied wine that also sometimes includes hints of gooseberry and black currant. In California, it is often called Fume Blanc, but it is New Zealand that produces some of the finest versions of this wine with a fruity style.

- **Sémillon**

This is the foundation of Sauternes and the dry white wines of Graves and Pessac-Léognan. It's a great late-harvest wine with complex notes of fig, tobacco, pear, and honey. It is used as a blending wine for adding body, flavor, and texture to Sauvignon Blanc, and it can also be blended with Chardonnay. For the latter, however, it doesn't add much to the flavor.

- **Sherry**

This is a fortified wine from southern Spain – specifically, the Jerez de la Frontera district. The main grape variety is Palomino, but Pedro Ximénez is used to produce sweeter, heavier wines. There are a number of styles, including Manzanilla, Fino, Amontillado, Oloroso, Pale Cream, Cream, Palo, and Pedro Ximénez. The drier varieties are best served chilled while the medium-sweet to sweet styles are better at room temperature.

- **Soave**

This delicate Muscat flavored wine has a very distinct flavor produced from the combination of Muscat of Alexandria and Grenache Gris grapes in 1948. It's a straw-colored dry, white wine that comes from Italy's Veneto region;

however, University of California, Davis makes a clone called symphony.

- **Tokay**

See Pinot Gris.

- **Traminer**

This is the German word for grapes. See Gewürztraminer.

- **Trebbiano**

This is found in almost any basic white Italian wine. It is actually a sanctioned ingredient in the blend that produces Chianti. It is produced in Italy and Ugni Blancin in France, but in France, it is often called St. Émilion, and it is used to make Cognac and Armagnac brandy.

- **Ugni Blanc**

See Trebbiano

- **Valpolicella**

This is a light, semi-dry red from the Veneto Region in Italy, and it is typical to drink it young.

- **Verdicchio**

This is an Italian white wine that is pale, light-bodied, and crisp.

- **Viognier**

Viognier is a very difficult grape to grow, but it produces a floral, spicy white wine that is medium to full-bodied and very fruity with peach and apricot aromas.

- **Zinfandel**

This wine can be bold and intense or light and fruity with predominantly raspberry flavors. It is a good wine for blending since it brings out flavors of cherry, wild berry, and plum with leather, earth, and tar notes. It is the grape most widely grown in California, the majority of which is turned into White Zinfandel, a blush, slightly sweet wine.

Now, with your favorite glass in hand, taste it again while reading the description! After all, this should be an interactive learning experience.

CHAPTER SUMMARY

In this chapter, we've covered the journey of the grape. Specifically, we've discussed the following topics:

- The maturation, pruning, training, budding, and harvesting of the vine;
- The fermentation of the grape into wine;
- The significance of wine throughout history in multiple cultures and religions;
- The main wine-producing nations;
- The wine varieties available.

In the next chapter, you'll discover the difference between Old World and New World wines.

CHAPTER TWO: OLD WORLD VERSUS NEW WORLD

It's time to fill up your glass again and learn about the old and the new. You have probably heard about Old World wines versus New World wines, but that exactly does that mean, and how does it affect the taste of your grape? Let's begin with the basics.

OLD VERSUS NEW

When you're talking about the Old World or the New World, these are geographical terms referring to the Americas and everywhere else. Basically, the New World is the world of the Americas – North, Central, and South America – discovered really by the Native Americans who lived there long before anyone arrived from Europe. The Americas were then rediscovered by Columbus as he sailed the ocean blue. So, the New World refers to the Americas and wines produced in any region within North, South, or Central America. Old World refers to every other part of the world – Europe, Asia, Africa, India, and anywhere else outside of the Americas. If a wine was made in California, it's New World, and if it's made in Italy, it's Old World. Argentina – New World, Spain – Old World, and so on. So, what about the wine in each?

Old World Winemaking Countries

While wine can be made anywhere that grapes can grow, the major winemaking countries in the Old World are the following:

- Austria
- France
- Germany
- Greece
- Hungary
- Italy
- Portugal
- Spain

THESE ARE THE COUNTRIES THAT HAVE BEEN IN THE winemaking business for a long time – centuries as opposed to decades. As a result, each of these countries has its own traditional wine laws, and these laws dictate which grapes can be grown in which regions, the minimum level of alcohol by volume for the various types of wine, and even the acceptable residual sugar content. The wines from the Old World are usually labeled according to the region in which they were produced. The reason for that is summed up in one word: *terroir*, which translates as "taste of place". The Old World winemakers assert that this refers to all of the other contributors to the wine flavor aside from the grape and the yeast – that means the soil type, the slope, aspect (the direction the slope faces), and the altitude. Those all contribute to the flavor of the wine, and Old World vintners believe that these factors are more influential on the wine flavor than even the grape itself. They consider it the grape to be the vessel in which the land expresses itself. So, how does the land express itself in each of the regions above? Let's take a look.

Austria: Though this is not a household name for wine, it has produced a prominent wine – Gruner Veltliner, which has a friendly flavor profile including a white peppery punch and – yes, this is an industry term – a kick-ass acidity. The regions of Austria where wine production is common include Wachau, known for Rieslings and Gruner Veltliner, Wagram, famous for a richer version of Gruner Veltliner and its cousin, Roter Veltliner, and Neusiedlersee (don't try to say that after your second glass of wine), which is known for its Noble Rot. The wines common to this region include the following:

Whites

- Gruner Veltliner: This is a wine that pairs great with some foods typically considered difficult to match for wines, like artichokes and asparagus. It has a piercing acidity that cuts through the richness of certain dishes like wiener schnitzels.
- Riesling: This wine is oilier and richer than the German and Alsatian varieties, but it is still bone dry.
- Mueller Thurgau: This is the product of a grape created in the lab – some like to call those Frankengrapes – and it is a Riesling Sylvaner cross the results in wines that go from simple to stellar.
- Pinot Blanc: This is often used for blending, but it can also produce a stellar wine that has a fresh, floral flavor when young and a zippy acidity. With a little age, it develops a lovely hazelnut, spicy component.

Reds

- Blaufränkisch: This is characterized by deep wood berry or cherry tones and a characteristic acidity. The wine had a dense structure and prominent tannins, and it ages well.
- Zweigelt: This is the most widely grown red grape in this region, and it is technically a cross between the Blaufränkisch and St. Laurent. It is lightweight, but it has a smooth, medium body with a black pepper finish.
- St. Laurent: This is Austria's version of a Pinot Noir, and it boasts a dark, sturdy, fruity, and piquant flavor with Morello cherry notes. It also ages well.

France: Of course French wines are some of the most famous in the world. And, France takes their reputation seriously. They strongly advocate for the concept of terroir, and the wines from each region must abide by certain rules. They have a rigid certification process that determines whether or not the wine can bear the regional name on the label, and their labels are famously complicated. The process is called the *appellation d'origine contrôlée*, and if you see this term on the label, you know the wine has passed the test for being typical of the region from which it comes. The regions of note include the following:

- **Alsace**: This area produces noble varieties such as Riesling, Pinot Gris, Pinot Blanc, Gewurztraminer, and Muscat.
- **Bordeaux**: This is the home of the meaty, sophisticated, age-worthy reds, whites, and dessert wines, such as Cabernet Sauvignon,

Cabernet Franc, Merlot, Sauvignon Blanc, and
Semillon.

- **Burgundy**: This is the home of the silkiest Pinot
  Noirs and the most enchanting Chardonnays.
- **Cahors**: This is where you'll find Malbec's more
  rustic, robust, and French cousin, the OG
  Malbec.
- **Champagne**: The name says it all. This is the
  birthplace of the bubbly and those produced here
  are incomparable.
- **Loire**: This region produces a variety of wines,
  from bone dry to sticky sweet to sparkling to
  rose, and everything in between. Chenin Blanc
  and Cabernet Franc are two varieties that are
  exceptional in this region.
- **Languedoc-Roussillon**: This is home to a variety
  of stellar reds – Minervois and Herault – and
  whites from Picpoul de Pinet.
- **Rhone Valley**: This is a well-known region that is
  split north to south. The north features
  exceptional whites from Viognier, Marsanne, and
  Roussanne and reds based on Syrah. The south,
  on the other hand, is full of tasty blends, such as
  those based on Grenache Blanc and some 14
  different varieties from Chateauneuf du Pape.
  You can also find well-priced alternatives here,
  including Vacqueyras and Gigondas, which sport
  a concentrated berry fruit, leathery earth, deep
  pepper spice flavor.
- **Provence**: This region produces rosés like no
  other region. They are fresh and delicious all year
  round. The region also boasts the reds of Bandol,
  which are deep, dark, and brooding.

Germany: German white wines are all about high acidity and produce stellar varieties. But, they do have a few good reds as well as their own contribution to the champagne family, the stellar Sekt. The grapes of note include the Riesling (anbaugebiete), Pinot Gris (Grauburgunder), Pinot Blanc (Weissburgunder), and Pinot Noir (Spatburgunder). Interestingly, Mosel, which is one of Germany's finest wine-producing regions, is technically too cold for winemaking. It is just north of 50 degrees latitude, so how do they do it? The vineyards are strategically designed to make use of every bit of sunlight. They are planted on steep terraces angled so that each plant will receive the sunlight it needs without blocking the other buds. And, the best vineyards overlook the Mosel River which reflects the sunlight onto the plants, thereby doubling the sunshine they receive.

Greece: This one of the most ancient winemaking regions in the world, but many people are unfamiliar with Greek wine varieties. They include wines made from the following grapes:

Whites

- Assyrtiko: Delicious, crisp, and dry, this wine is from the isle of Santorini.
- Moschofilero: This pink-skinned variety yields full, aromatic wines.
- Roditis: This can vary in flavor depending on where it is grown, but it is excellent at transmitting terroir.

Reds

- Agiorghitiko: This is the Greek version of

Cabernet Franc or Merlot. It is smooth, fresh, and has a delicious berry and herbal flavor.

- Xinomavro: This wine is similar to a robust, It Italian Nebbiolo. It is rich in tannins and high in acidity, making it anything but subtle.

Hungary: As far as winemaking goes, Hungary is most famous for the sweet wines of Tokaj. They are rich and honeyed with wild, high-toned acidity. The typical international varieties include Cabernet Sauvignon, Cabernet Franc, Merlot, Sauvignon Blanc, Chardonnay, and more. The indigenous wine varieties include the following:

Whites

- Furmint: This is the dominant Hungarian grape, and it is well-known for producing Tokaji, the Botrytised (i.e., affected by the fungus *Botrytis cinerea*) sweet wine that Hungary is most known for; it also, however, produces both stellar dry and sparkling wines.
- Hárslevelu: This name of this grape means linden leaf in Hungarian, and it lives up to its name with a delicate floral flavor. It is commonly blended with Furmint to produce both dry and Botrytised sweet wines.
- Irsai Oliver: This is a cross of some more obscure indigenous varieties which possess a muscat panache.
- Juhfark: This word means sheep's tail, but the wine it produces is rich and fiery. It comes from the Somlo region of Hungary.

Reds

- Kadarka: This was Hungary's most common grape prior to the second world war, but it has since become rarer. It has the fresh flavor of a Beaujolais with darker fruit and a more tannic bit.
- Kékfrankos: This is a highly acidic wine that combines brambly blue and black fruit with sweet pepper spice flavors.
- Kékoportó: The Kék prefix to the name means blue, and it indicates the blue fruit flavors common in this variety. This grape has the capacity to produce very high yields but at the expense of the wine quality.

The regions of note in Hungary include Somlo, known for its fiery whites produced in rich volcanic soil, Villany, one of the largest regions that produces a wide variety of grapes, both indigenous and international, Eger, which is home of the Bull's Blood legend that asserts that Hungarian troops were victorious over Turkish soldiers because they mixed their wine with bull's blood – the wines from the region, however, are rich and velvety, not bloody – and Tokaj, home of Hungary's famous sweet wines.

Italy: The list here is a long one – too long to cover everything here. Suffice it to say that there are numerous exceptional, stellar wines produced in this country. The main regions include Piedmont where Nebbiolo is well-known, Lombardy where Franciacorta is produced, Trentino-Sudtirol known for some unusual grapes like Muller-Thurgau and Kerner (whites), and Lagrein and Pinot Nero (reds), and Friuli-Venezia Giulia, known for its international and indigenous varieties including Cabernet Sauvignon and Schiopetino. There's also Emilia-Romagna which produces the sparkling red Lambrusco, Veneto, the homeland of

Bardolino, Valpolicella, and Amarone blends, Marche which produces Verdicchio, Abruzzi, home of a great red, Montepulciano d'Abruzzo, and Puglia, home of Negroamaro and Primitivo, two good value reds. This list is not complete without also mentioning Sicily, known for Marsala wines, Umbria, home of Sagrantino di Montefalco – a stellar red, Tuscany, which produces red varieties from Sangiovese including Chianti, Brunello di Montalcino, and Vino Nobile di Montepulciano, and finally, Liguria, home of Cinqueterre, a Vermentino based wine with a bright acidity that pairs well with deep-fried seafood. That's a long list, but I'm quite sure you recognize several of the wines mentioned.

Portugal: Portugal is mostly famous for fortified wines – or Ports – which are sweet, rich, and complex dessert wines. These include Tawny, Ruby, White Port, Late Bottle Vintage, Crusted, Vintage Port, and Single Quinta Vintage Port. Additionally, the island of Madeira makes purposefully baked, fortified wines including Rainwater, Sercial, Verdelho, Bual, and Malmsey. The country also produces some delicious, affordable table wines as well, including Vinho Verde, Lourinho, and Dao.

Spain: One of the most well-known Spanish wines is Rioja, but there are more notable wines produced in this region of the world. They include the delicious sparkling wine Cava, which mimics the Methode Traditionelle of Champagne, and the following whites and reds:

Whites

- Godello: This grape was almost extinct in the 1970s, but a few determined winemakers couldn't let it go, and today it is frequently likened to Chardonnay for its neutral character. That makes it an exceptional wine for blending.

- Txakoli: This is a Basque country wine, which is dry, low in alcohol, and heavy in minerals. For that reason, it should be consumed when young.
- Viura: This is the white version of Rioja. It's a sturdy grape called Macabeo in other parts of Spain where it is frequently used to make Cava. The best of these wines has a medium to high acidity, a delicate floral aroma, and a creaminess on the palate.

Reds

- Tempranillo: This is the grape known for making Rioja, but it also produces a deeper, earthier wine called Ribera del Duero.
- Grenache: This is known as Garnacha in Spain, and it is typically used as a blending grape in Rioja. It can, however, also produce – on its own – Navarro and Priorat, which have juicy, fresh, spicy and stellar flavors.

Finally, there is also a fortified dessert wine produced in Spain known as Sherry. It ranges from dry to almost salty and to sticky sweet and caramelized. It is produced using the Solera method that blends different vintages together to produce a consistent signature house style.

New World Winemaking Countries

THE MAIN NEW WORLD WINEMAKING COUNTRIES include the following:

- United States
- Argentina
- Mexico
- Canada
- Chile

While indigenous peoples in the New World made alcoholic beverages from various plants including maize and quinoa, they did not make wine. Because wines transported during the voyages of discovery were not brought in sealed bottles, they were prone to sour. Thus, it wasn't until the second voyage of Columbus in 1494 that the first attempts to grow grapevines began in Hispaniola. From those early beginnings, the industry has grown in the Americas to include the fifth largest wine producer, Argentina. Let's take a look at what these countries have to offer.

United States: Though most states in the US produce some wine, some 90 percent of American wine comes from the states of California, Washington State, and Oregon. The vineyards in California were started by the Spanish missionaries after Europeans arrived in the Americas. Later, grapes were brought by immigrants from Bordeaux and Italy who brought their native grapes with them. The United States banned alcohol between 1920 -1923 during a time now called Prohibition, which stopped the thriving wine industry in its tracks. One consequence of Prohibition was that the vineyards were then replanted with lower quality grapes, and that has resulted in a change in taste preferences from dry to much sweeter styles. The industry started to recover in the late 1960s and 1970s when wine pioneers such as Ernest and Julio Gallo and Robert Mondavi began to reinvent the local styles. A few of the styles include the following:

Whites

- Fumé Blanc: This is a dry, heavily oaked style that represents Mondavi's reinvention of Sauvignon Blanc. It's made from the same green-skinned grape as Sauvignon Blanc, and has flavors that boast a lime blossom and grapefruit citrus with green apple, peach, melon, and just a hint of jasmine.
- White Zinfandel: This black-skinned grape is grown in over 10 percent of California vineyards. It's genetically equivalent to the Primitivo variety grown in Italy, and tends to have light, citrus flavors, such as orange, strawberry, and cherry.
- Chardonnay: This green-skinned grape variety originated in Burgundy, and tastes differently depending on where it's grown and how it's

made. It frequently has a dry, medium to full-bodied citrus flavor with lemon, papaya, and pineapple and moderate acidity. When aged with oak, it shows notes of vanilla.

- Viognier: The central coast of California is the leading producer of this variety with over 2,000 acres (809 hectares) of the grape planted there. The California version of this wine is noticeably higher in alcohol as compared to other wines from the same grape. It's best paired with seafood.

Reds

- Pinot Noir: These tend to be produced in the northwest United States and have flavors ranging from a sweet black cherry to black raspberry with secondary aromas of vanilla, clover, coca-cola, and caramel. Oregon Pinot Noir is usually lighter in color and texture than that produced in California. It's also often more tart.
- Cabernet Sauvignon: The Napa Valley version has a cherry pit, orange rind, and slate-like minerality with flavors of currants, cherries, orange rind, and a note of earthiness.
- Insignia: This wine boasts aromas of carpaccio, black cherries, cassis, blackberries, black cardamom, and maduro cigar tobacco, and the flavors are acid-zipped with lingering notes of violets, sandalwood, tobacco, and pencil shavings.
- Quintessa: This is a brooding wine with flavors of tar, black licorice, camphor, and black plums as

well as peppercorn. It also has notes of baking spices, star anise, and dried flowers.

Argentina: Argentina is currently the fifth biggest wine producer with a long tradition of winemaking under the Spanish, but the industry has also been influenced by recent Italian and German immigrants. As a result of the long history of viticulture, Argentina has experienced the evolution of several local varieties, the most typical of which is the Torrontes grape which produces an aromatic white wine. Among their reds, Malbec has been their most successful variety. The main winemaking regions include the Mendoza Province, San Juan, Salta, La Rioja, Catamarca, Rio Negro, and Buenos Aires. To use the grape name on the label, by law, 100 percent of the wine must be made by that grape variety.

Some of the more prominent wines include the following:

- Malbec
- Bonarda
- Cabernet Sauvignon
- Syrah
- Tempranillo
- Barbera
- Dolcetto
- Freisa
- Lambrusco
- Nebbiolo
- Raboso
- Sangiovese

Mexico: Mexico is actually the oldest winemaking region

in the Americas. Spanish explorers and settlers settled in the fertile valley in the state of Coahuila in 1549. By 1597, the Hacienda de San Lorenzo was established, and there, Spanish settler Don Lorenzo Garcia founded the Casa Madero, the oldest winery house in the Americas. Many of the varieties grown there and in other parts of Mexico were exported to California and other areas of what was then Northern New Spain. In 2013, close to 90 percent of Mexican wine was produced in the state of Baja California. Some of the best wines include the following:

Reds

- Cabernet Sauvignon
- Zinfandel
- Cabernet Franc
- Carignan
- Grenache
- Merlot
- Malbec
- Syrah
- Petit Verdot
- Tempranillo
- Nebbiolo
- Dolcetto
- Barbera
- Petite Sirah
- Pinot Noir

Whites

- Chardonnay
- Chasselas

- Chenin Blanc
- Macabeo
- Muscat Blanc
- Palomino
- Riesling
- Semillon
- Sauvignon Blanc
- Viognier

Canada: Canada had a similar winemaking history as the eastern United States. They attempted early on to grow *Vitis vinifera*, but later developed a significant export wine industry based on *Vitis labrusca* and *Vitis riparia*. The country also had its own Prohibition which lasted until 1927, and the consequences of that inhibited the wine industry until 1974. After that time, the improved grape varieties and viticulture practices brought an expansion of the wine industry, which centers around parts of southern Ontario where the land is warmed by the Great Lakes. Southern British Columbia is another major winemaking region. They have made great progress with red wines from Bordeaux varieties and Pinot Noir, but by far, their most successful wines are ice wines made from such grape varieties as Riesling, Vidal, and Cabernet Franc.

Chile: Like Argentina, the winemaking in Chile dates back to the Spanish conquest. In the 19th century, Bordeaux varieties arrived in the country, and Carmenere has become one of the signature grapes in Chile. Chile is now the seventh biggest wine-producing country in the world. Chilean vineyards have traditionally been in semi-arid areas irrigated by high altitude Andean waters, but in recent years, cooler areas, such as the Leyda Valley famed for its Pinot Noir and the Bio-Bio Valley which boasts Riesling and Gewurztraminer,

have been planted with great success. Chile is also famously
free of phylloxera, a sap-sucking insect that feeds on the roots
and leaves of grapevines. This insect destroyed most of the
vineyards in Europe in the late 19th century.

Other Wine Producing Countries of Note

There are a few other countries – outside of the European
region and the Americas – that are emerging or have become
established as growing winemaking regions. These include
the following:

- Australia
- South Africa
- New Zealand
- China

Australia: The first vine cuttings arrived in Australia
from South Africa in 1788. The first Australian wine exports
began in 1822, and by the 1880s, Australia was winning
prizes for its wine in Europe. Many vineyards were destroyed,
however, in a phylloxera plague that hit in the 1870s, but
southern Australia was free of the insect, and as a result, it
now boasts some of the oldest continuously growing vineyards on the planet. Their vineyards now are increasingly
planted in cooler areas, such as Tasmania, famed for its Pinot
Noir. Additionally, several regional specialties have emerged,
such as Shiraz in the Barossa Valley, Cabernet Sauvignon in
Coonawarra, and Semillon in the Hunter Valley. The fortified wines in Rutherglen are also considered the finest among
the countries colonized in the voyages of discovery.

South Africa: The founder of Cape Town, Richard
Cavendish, was also the first person to produce wine in
South Africa. He began doing so in 1659, and by the late
18th century, theSouth African wine called Constantia,

which was made from Muscat de Frontignan, became popular among the European Royalty. The South African vineyards were wiped out by phylloxera, however, and the wines produced following that were of lower quality. The end of apartheid brought a renewed interest in investing and innovating the vineyards around Cape Town. The regions that produce some world-class wines include Paarl, Colombard, and Stellenbosch. They produce Bordeaux varieties including Shiraz and a Pinotage variety bred locally from Pinot Noir and Cinsaut. South Africa has also become the second home of Chenin Blanc, which prior to the mid-20th century was known as Steen. The country is also once again producing Constantia.

New Zealand: The birth of New Zealand's viticulture came by way of Croatian immigrants at the end of the 19th century. It didn't flourish, however, until the 1970s. Various grape varieties were tried, but in the 1980s New Zealand developed their own distinctive style of Sauvignon Blanc, and that has since become their trademark. They also now grow Burgundy grapes of Chardonnay and Pinot Noir in the southerly vineyards with great success. There has also recently been an increasing popularity of 'aromatic' white varieties like Riesling and Gewurztraminer.

China: Unbeknownst to many a wine connoisseur, winemaking actually has a long history in China. It has been over-shadowed by the production of other alcoholic beverages, such as *huangjiu* and *baijiu*. Since the economic reforms of the 1980s, wine consumption, however, has grown dramatically, and China is now among the top ten global markets for wine. The most notable winemaking regions include Beijing, Ningxia, Yantai, Zhangjiakou in Hebei, Yibin in Sichuan, Tonghua in Jilin, and Taiyuan in Shanxi. The largest winemaking region is Yantai-Penglai, which boasts over 140 wineries and produces 40 percent of China's wine. One of the most notable Chinese wines is a Cabernet Sauvignon blend. It won the Decanter World Wine Award international trophy for wines in its price class in 2009. Wine experts were astonished and even questioned the veracity of the origin of the wine. In 2011, experts from China and France blind-tasted five wines from each of the two regions of Bordeaux and Ningxia. The competition was called, "Bordeaux against Ningxia," and four out of five of the top wines were from Ningxia. Thus, China is becoming one of the better wine-making countries.

What are the Differences Between New and Old World Wines?

Now that you're all caught up on the major wine-producing countries around the world, you might be wondering what exactly is the difference between Old World and New World wines? The answer is that there are three main differences. Let's look at each.

1. Naming Wines

Old World: The name comes from the location where the wine is made. For example, a wine made from the Malbec grape in the Cahors region of France would be called Cahors rather than Malbec.

New World: The name of the wine is taken from the name of the grape used to produce it. A wine made in Mendoza, Argentina from a Malbec grape is called Malbec rather than Mendoza.

2. The Process

Old World: It's all about tradition in the Old world. There, winemakers must adhere to very strict regulations. Wine has been made a certain way for centuries, and the regulations require those be maintained.

New World: Winemakers in the New World are free to experiment more than their Old World counterparts. They don't have to confront the strict regulations present in the Old World, and therefore, they can try different combinations and new technologies.

3. Taste

Old World: Wines from the Old World tend to be leaner, higher in acidity, and contain more tannins.

New World: The wines made in the New World tend to taste richer, have bolder fruit flavors, and just in general, have a more "polished" taste.

Well, now that you're all caught up on the difference between the Old World and the New World, it's time to learn more about the grape itself. Did you know that grapes are quite the characters? Read on to find out more.

Chapter Summary

In this chapter, we've discussed the difference between the Old World and the New World with regard to winemaking. Specifically, we've covered the following topics:

- Definitions for Old World and New World;
- The major wine-producing regions in the Old World;
- The major wine-producing regions in the New World;

- Other emerging wine-producing regions;
- The difference between Old World and New World wines.

IN THE NEXT CHAPTER, YOU'LL DISCOVER THE character of the grape.

CHAPTER THREE: GRAPES HAVE QUITE THE CHARACTER

Another chapter, and you know what that means, another glass of your favorite wine. It's time now to examine the grapes and their character, but first, it's a good idea to understand what that means, so let's begin with definitions.

CHARACTER

When referring to wine, character is used in three main ways:

1. ***Quality***: Character can be used to mean a quality wine with distinctive qualities; something that is instantly identifiable because it has a unique personality and complex flavors;

2. ***Style/Weight***: You might, for example, say that a wine is light in character, which can mean it lacks character or that its flavors are more subtle. The term can also refer directly to the weight of the wine, which refers to the alcohol content. Light-bodied wines are typically lower in alcohol and described as crisp or fresh.

3. ***Taste/Smell***: Character is also used to describe the specific tastes or smells, such as in the example, "The wine has nutty characters."

The characters of wine are created by the combination of the grape variety, the terroir, the climate, and the specific winemaking techniques employed by the vintner. Though some wines may have similar characters, no two wines will be exactly the same in this regard, and they are affected by a number of factors that include the following:

- **Terroir**: This the contribution the soil makes to the fruit, and subsequently, the wine. Because of terroir, a Sauvignon Blanc produced in Chile will have a different character than one from Italy or France.

- **Grape variety**: Each grape variety has its own character that it imparts to the wine.
- **Climate**: The amount of sun, rain, wind, or snow that a vine receives will produce a different character. That's why wines from different years have different character profiles.
- **Winemaking techniques**: This refers to the oak, the fermentation period, and the blend, all of which have a significant effect on the final character profile.

Character Terminology

Before discussing specific grape characters, let's look at the terms used to describe character. This is where you learn what earthy means!

- Acidic: This describes wines with a high total acid content that results in a tart or sour flavor and a sharp edge on your palate.
- Aeration: This is the process of letting the wine breathe, and it's why you swirl it in your glass before tasting it. It lets in air, but it's debatable whether that actually improves the taste. It can soften young, tannic wines, but fatigue older ones.
- Aftertaste: This refers to those tastes that linger in the mouth after tasting the wine. It's also referred to as the finish, and it's the single, most important factor in judging a wine's character. Great wines are described as having a rich, long, complex aftertaste.
- Aggressive: This refers to wines that are

unpleasantly harsh in taste or texture, typically because of high levels of tannins or acid.

- Alcoholic: This describes wine that has too much alcohol for its body and weight. Such a wine is said to be unbalanced, and it will taste too heavy or hot as a result. This particular quality is noticeable in the aroma and aftertaste.
- Appearance: This refers to the wine's clarity rather than its color.
- Aroma: This refers to the smell the wine acquires from the grapes and the fermentation process. It can also be used to mean the total smell that includes changes resulting from oak aging or after bottling. Bouquet is another term used for this.
- Astringent: This refers to a rough, harsh taste that puckers your mouth, usually because of high tannin levels or acidity. It is more common in red wines, and when the harshness is notable, the wine is described as astringent.
- Austere: This term describes a hard, high acid wine that lacks depth and roundness. It's typically a descriptor applied to young wines that need to soften or those wines that lack richness and body.
- Awkward: This is a wine that has poor structure, meaning it is clumsy or unbalanced.
- Backbone: This refers to wines that are full-bodied, well-structured, and balanced by a desirable level of acidity.
- Backward: This describes a young wine that is less developed than others of the same type and class from the same vintage.
- Balance: When the elements of the wine are harmonious and no single element dominates, the wine is said to have balance.

- Bite: This refers to a wine that has a marked degree of tannin or acidity. An acid grip in the finish would ideally be a zestful tang, and this is typically tolerable only in a rich, full-bodied wine.
- Bitter: This is one of the four basic tastes, along with sour, salty, and sweet. Some grapes, like Gewurztraminer and Muscat, have a bitter edge to their flavors. Tannins and stems are sources of bitterness, and if the bitter quality is dominant in the wine's flavor or aftertaste, it is considered a fault. A trace of bitterness in sweet wines can complement the flavors, but in young, red wines, it's often a warning signal since it tends not to dissipate with age. Most fine, mature wines should not be bitter on the palate.
- Blunt: This refers to a wine that has a strong, and often alcoholic, flavor, but which is lacking in aromatic interest and development on the palate.
- Body: This is the impression of fullness the wine leaves on the palate, usually because of a combination of glycerin, alcohol, and sugar. Wines are commonly described as full-bodied, medium-bodied or medium-weight, or light-bodied.
- Bottle Sickness: This refers to a temporary condition whereby the wine has a muted or disjointed fruit flavor. It typically occurs right after bottling or if the wine (particularly fragile wines) is shaken in travel. It's also called bottle shock, and a few days of rest will fix it right up.
- Bouquet: This refers to the smell a wine develops after it has been bottled and aged. It's most often

used to describe mature wines that have developed more complex flavors.

- Brawny: This describes wines that are hard, intense, tannic with raw, woody flavors. The term elegant is the opposite to this descriptor.
- Briary: This describes wines with an earthy or stemmy wild berry character.
- Bright: This term refers to fresh, ripe, zesty, lively young wines that have vivid, focused flavors.
- Brilliant: This is used to describe very clear wines with zero visible suspended, particulate matter. It isn't always a good sign since it can mean the wine is highly filtered.
- Browning: This refers to the wine's color, and it typically indicates the wine is mature and might be faded. It's a particularly bad sign for young wines, but less significant in older wines. Wines that are 20 to 30 years old can have a brownish edge, but still be quite enjoyable.
- Burnt: This refers to wine with an overdone, smoky, toasty, or singed edge, and it is used to describe overripe grapes.
- Buttery: This indicates the wine smells of melted butter or a toasty oak. It can also be used to refer to texture. For example, a Chardonnay might be described as rich and buttery.
- Cedary: This refers to the smell of cedarwood that occurs in mature Cabernet Sauvignons or Cabernet blends that have been aged in French or American oak.
- Chewy: This describes a rich, heavy, tannic wine that is full-bodied.
- Cigar Box: This is another descriptor that indicates a cedar aroma.

- Clean: This refers to a wine that is fresh on the palate and free of any off-taste. But, it doesn't always imply a good quality.
- Closed: Wines described as closed are concentrated and have character, but they don't have much in the way of aroma or flavor.
- Cloudiness: This refers to a lack of clarity in a wine. It can be fine if the wine is older and has sediment, but it can be a sign of protein instability, yeast spoilage, or re-fermentation in the bottle if the wine is younger.
- Coarse: This refers to texture, and particularly, those wines with excessive tannins or oak. It can also describe sparkling wines with harsh bubbles.
- Complexity: This is an element of all great wines, and it describes a combination of richness, depth, flavor intensity, focus, balance, harmony, and finesse.
- Corked: This describes wines with a musty, moldy flavor and aroma, and a dry aftertaste, that results from a tainted cork.
- Decanting: This is the process for separating the wine from its sediment prior to drinking. It is achieved by slowly, carefully pouring wine from the bottle into a decanter.
- Delicate: This describes a light to medium-bodied wine with good flavors. It is desirable in certain wines, including Pinot Noir and Riesling.
- Dense: This describes a wine with concentrated aromas on the nose and palate, and it is a good sign in a young wine.
- Depth: This refers to the complexity and concentration of flavors in a win. It is the opposite of shallow.

- Dirty: This refers to any and all foul smells that can occur in wines, particularly those with bad barrels or corks. This is a sign of poor winemaking.
- Dry: A dry wine has no perceptible taste of sugar. The majority of wine tasters will perceive sugar at levels of 0.5 to 0.7 percent, so a dry wine would have lower levels than that.
- Drying Out: This refers to losing fruit or sweetness in wines to the point where acid, alcohol, or tannin dominate the taste. By this stage, the wine will not improve.
- Earthy: Here it is!! The term you've been waiting for! Earthy, when used as a positive term, refers to pleasant, clean qualities that add complexity to the aroma and flavors. When used as a negative term, it refers to a funky, barnyard character that crossed into dirtiness.
- Elegant: Wines of grace, balance, and beauty are described as elegant.
- Fat: Fat wines are those that are full-bodied, high in alcohol, and low in acidity. They give a fat impression on the palate, which can be a plus if they also have bold, ripe, rich flavors. It can also be a negative, however, suggesting that the wine's structure is suspect.
- Finish: This is the key to judging the wine's quality. It's a measure of the taste that lingers in the mouth after the wine is tasted. Great wines are considered to have rich, long, complex finishes.
- Fleshy: A wine that has a soft, smooth texture with very little tannin.
- Flinty: This is used to describe extremely dry

white wines like Sauvignon Blanc, the bouquet of which connotes flint struck against steel.

- Floral (Flowery): This means the wine has the aroma of flowers. It's a term that's mostly used for white wines.
- Fresh: This is used to describe wines with a lively, clean, and fruity character. It's essential in young wines.
- Fruity: This simply means having the aroma or taste of fruits.
- Grapey: This describes a wine that has simple flavors and aromas that are associated with fresh table grapes as compared to the complex fruit flavors associated with fine wines.
- Grassy: This is a signature descriptor used for Sauvignon Blanc, and it is a plus unless the wine is overbearing and pungent.
- Green: This refers to tasting like unripe fruit. Wines that are made from grapes that aren't ripe will possess this quality. It can be pleasant as with Rieslings and Gewurztraminers.
- Grip: This refers to a texture that is pleasantly firm, often due to tannin. This gives definition to certain wines, such as Cabernet and Port.
- Hard: This is a quality that results from high acidity or tannins, and it is often used to describe young, red wines. It's synonymous with firm.
- Harmonious: This refers to a well-balanced wine with no components lacking.
- Harsh: This describes astringent wines high in alcohol or tannins.
- Hazy: A hazy wine has small amounts of visible matter, and can describe a good quality of wine that is unfiltered.

- Hearty: This describes a full, warm, quality found in red wines high in alcohol.
- Heady: This describes high-alcohol wines.
- Herbaceous: This describes a wine with an aroma of herbs, and it is a plus in wines such as Sauvignon Blanc. Herbal is a synonym for this quality.
- Hot: Wines that are high in alcohol and unbalanced tend to burn with "heat" on the finish, and these are called hot. It's an acceptable quality in Port-style wines.
- Leafy: This refers to a wine that has a slightly herbaceous, vegetal quality that reminds one of leaves. It can be either a positive or a negative depending on whether it adds to the wine's flavor or detracts from it.
- Lean: Wines made in austere style are often described in a positive way as lean, but it can also be used to negatively indicate that a wine is lacking in fruit.
- Legs: This refers to viscous droplets that will form and slide down the sides of a glass when you swirl the wine.
- Length: This refers to the amount of time the taste and smell sensations persist after swallowing, and the longer they do, the better the wine.
- Lingering: If a wine aftertaste remains on the palate for several seconds, it is said to be lingering.
- Lively: This is used to describe wines that are fresh and fruity, bright and vivacious.
- Lush: This term describes wines with high residual sugar that produces a soft, viscous taste.

- Nose: This is the aroma character of wine, and it is also called aroma and includes the bouquet.
- Nouveau: A nouveau wine is light, fruity, youthful, and red. It has been bottled and sold as soon as possible, and the term is used mainly for Beaujolais.
- Nutty: This describes oxidized wines, and is often a flaw, but if it is close to an oaky flavor, it can be a plus.
- Oaky: This refers to an aroma or taste that is imparted to the wine by the oak barrels or casks in which it was aged. The term can be positive or negative with positive additional descriptors being toasty, vanilla, dill, cedary, and smoky while negative additional descriptors include charred, burnt, green cedar, lumber, and plywood.
- Off-Dry: This refers to a wine that is slightly sweet with a barely perceptible sugar content of 0.6 to 1.4 percent.
- Malic: This describes a green apple flavor that is found in young grapes, which diminishes as they ripen and mature.
- Meaty: This refers to red wines that are concentrated and have a chewy quality, qualities that often produce an aroma of cooked meat.
- Musty: This refers to a moldy or mildew smell, and it results from wine that is made from moldy grapes, wine stored in poorly cleaned tanks and barrels, and wine contaminated by a poor cork.
- Peak: This is the time that wine tastes its best, and it is a subjective quality.
- Perfumed: This term refers to a strong, sweet, floral aroma typical of some white wines.

- Pruny: This is a term that describes a flavor of overripe, dried-out grapes. If the flavor is in the right dose, it can add complexity to the wine.
- Raisiny: This simply refers to a taste of raisins that is produced from overripe grapes. In some wines, small doses of a raisiny taste can be pleasant.
- Raw: This refers to a young and undeveloped wine that is high in tannins, alcohol, or acidity. It's often a descriptor used to describe barrels samples of red wine.
- Rich: This common term refers to wines with a generous, full, pleasant flavor that is usually sweet and round in nature. Richness can be created by high levels of alcohol or glycerin, complex flavors, and an oaky vanilla character. When sweet wines are also backed up by fruity, ripe flavors, they are also described as rich.
- Robust: This means full-bodied, intense, and vigorous. It could also mean a bit overblown.
- Rustic: This refers to wines made by old-fashioned techniques or the tasting of wines from an earlier era. It can be a positive quality in those wines that require aging, but it can also be a negative descriptor for wines that are young and earthy but which should be fresh and fruity.
- Smoky: This describes an oak barrel byproduct – a smoky quality – that adds flavor and aromatic complexity to the wine.
- Soft: This describes wines low in tannin or acid or both, which makes it easy to drink.
- Spicy: This refers to the presence of spicy flavors like anise, cinnamon, cloves, mint, or pepper. These are frequently present in complex wines.

- Structure: This is a descriptor that is applied to the interaction of elements like acid, tannin, glycerin, alcohol, and body in the mouth. A structured wine has a texture feel in the mouth. This term is usually accompanied by modifiers, like "firm structure," or, "lacking in structure."
- Subtle: This refers to a delicate wine with finesse, which means understated flavors. It is a positive characteristic.
- Supple: This describes the texture of mostly red wines as it relates to tannin, body, and oak. This is a positive characteristic.
- Tannin: This refers to those substances found mostly in red wines that cause your mouth to pucker. It is a characteristic that mostly comes from grape skins, seeds, and stems, but it can also come from oak barrels. Tannin acts as a natural preservative that helps wine age.
- Tart: This refers to a sharp taste produced by high acidity.
- Tight: This refers to the wine's structure, concentration, and body. For example, one might describe a wine as, "tightly wound." Closed and compact are similar terms.
- Tinny: This simply refers to a metallic taste.
- Tired: This means the wine is limp, feeble, or lackluster.
- Toasty: This describes the flavor derived from oak barrels in which wines are aged, and it is also a character that can develop in sparkling wines.
- Vegetal: This refers to wines that smell or taste in a way that is reminiscent of plants and vegetables. In some wines, like Cabernet Sauvignon, a small amount of a vegetal quality is part of the varietal

character. If the vegetal element is dominant, however, or if it is in wines that shouldn't have a vegetal taste, those wines are considered flawed. This quality is caused by a chemical that makes wines smell like either asparagus or bell peppers.

- Velvety: This refers to wines that have a rich flavor and a silky, sumptuous texture.
- Vinous: The term means "winelike," and it is applied to dull wines that don't have a distinct varietal character.
- Volatile: This term is used to describe an excessive, undesirable amount of acidity that gives the wine a slightly sour, vinegary edge. When it occurs at levels below 0.1 percent, it is undetectable, but higher levels are considered a major defect.

Now that you're up on your character descriptions, let's look at the characters of specific grapes.

Grape Varietal Characters

You frequently hear the word character used with some kind of adjective – for example, nutty character – and there are different terms that can be used as descriptors, but let's take a look at the common grape varieties and the main aroma and taste characteristics associated with each of them.

White Grape Variety Characters

- **Chardonnay**: Chardonnays are typically full-
  bodied with fruit flavors that range from crisp,
  flinty apple and lemon to lush stone-fruit
  characters of peach and apricot. It can also have a
  ripe tropical fruit character that includes mango
  and pineapple. Some of the other key characters
  of Chardonnay depend on the yeast character and
  the aging. For example, many Chardonnays
  handle oak aging well – it gives the wine an oaky,
  spicy, burned character to varying degrees
  depending on the nature and age of the oak as
  well as the degree of toasting. The utilization of
  whole bunch pressing along with careful
  attention juice contact with the skin, stem, and
  pip (grape seed) will affect the tannins level.
  Chardonnays typically are described as ripe,
  structured, and not harsh in this regard. Finally,
  some Chardonnays will have a subtle, positive

earthy character and malolactic fermentation gives them a butter feel, which adds to the body of the wine.

- **Sauvignon Blanc**: These wines range in taste from a sharp flinty to green flavor to a fruity gooseberry and tropical fruit (melons and passion fruit) when they are more ripe. Cold-fermented Sauvignon Blancs typically have fresh fruity characters of lime and tropical fruit, and with less aging, they take on more body, complexity, and texture. Oak flavors will also add another dimension of complexity. Typical character descriptors for this varietal include herbaceous (herbal), cut grass, vegetal, and fruity – lemon, limes, grapefruit, gooseberry, tropical fruit (passionfruit and melon), canned peas, and asparagus.

- **Riesling**: These varietals are intensely scented with citrus aroma of lemons and limes. Increased complexity adds spicy characters with a hint of orange and honey. Residual sweetness is an important element for the balanced, tight, and strong acid that is typical for this grape variety. As it matures, a Riesling frequently takes on more of a honey and caramel character that adds complexity and intensity. Rieslings are typically lower in alcohol and emphasize the fruit kick.

- **Chenin Blanc**: This is often a fruity (melon and pineapple) varietal with elements of lanolin and wet wool characters. The grape yields a wine that is naturally high in acid, but this is compensated for by not fermenting it to dryness in order to maintain some residual sweetness. As this wine matures, it develops a whole new suite of nuance characters including a honey richness and an increased complexity of fruit characters.

- **Pinot Gris**: This wine has a similar weight and richness as Chardonnay, but it also has a spicy character similar to Gewurztraminer. The typical fruit character is pear and apple, but it also has a touch of cloves and spice. Sometimes it has some wood notes, but usually, this is very subtle and does not overpower the equally subtle fruit flavors.

- **Viognier**: This grape comes from the northern Rhone region in France, and it has an exotic, perfumed character with substantial stone fruit richness, usually peach and apricot. It also frequently has aromas and flavors that suggest pears, spices, and floral notes. It is frequently seasoned in oak barrels which impart another suite of characters that include richness and constrained acidity. It can be both a dry or an off-dry style depending on the fruit character quality and seasonal nuances.

- **Gewurztraminer**: This is one of the distinctive wine styles. It has aromas and flavors that include gingerbread, black pepper, lychees, cinnamon, cloves, and mint. Quality wines of this variety are typically made from low-yielding vineyards where leaf plucking and maturity help to avoid the need for the skin to provide richness and complexity. The stone fruit character comes out with exceptional intensity, which adds to the myriad of distinctive characteristics.

- **Semillon**: This grape variety is similar in many ways to Sauvignon Blanc in that it has a zingy acidity with tropical fruit characters. It is, in fact, frequently blended with Sauvignon Blanc for complexity and length, which can result in stunningly rich, sweet wines because of the susceptibility to "noble rot". Noble rot refers to the beneficial effect of the grey fungus, *Botrytis cinerea*. The variety is from Graves, and it is the basis of intense, rich, sweet wines.

- **Verdelho**: This grape variety preserves its acidity in hotter climates and has lemon and stone fruit characters often encased in honey and nutty richness. It also frequently includes hints of pear and spice when the vineyard is managed well and the wine is fermented in a barrel.

- **Muscat**: This includes a wide family of grapes that are distinctive for their musky, sweet, grape flavor. They are often blended with other grapes to yield a perfumed character. Other characters include lemony, appley, lively flavors with floral notes. Often, orange hints are evidence as well.

- **Marsanne**: This is a new grape varietal that also helps increase the popularity of the Rhone-style wines in California and the United States. The likely origin is the northern Rhone. It has great productivity and intriguingly unique aromas. It has become the popular choice for blending, even more so than the traditional Roussanne varieties. Aside from the plantings in California, this variety is also grown in less than 250 acres in Australia, and some of those date back a century or more. Because of the way the grapes hang on this vine, the fruit is susceptible to a powdery mildew called odium, bunch rot, berry cracking, and excessive juicing. The wine produced by this varietal is medium-gold to amber in color, fairly full-bodied, and described as almost waxy. If the growing conditions are right, the aromas include almond paste or citrus mixed with perfume and model airplane cement. Because the varietal is low in acid, the wine is best consumed young.

- **Roussanne**: This varietal is not a very cooperative vine, and many vintners would rather work with other varietals. It gives an irregular yield and tends toward uneven and late ripening. It also has little resistance to odium and rot, and it is easily damaged by wind and drought. The only reason it survives today is because of its unique aroma and bracing acidity. The name comes from its light brownish, russet cast from ripe berries. It is from the Rhone region in France, and it is also grown in the Châteauneuf-du-Pape area to the south as well as a few other areas in Italy and Australia. It is not often bottled on its own in Europe because it can be thin and tart, but it is instead frequently blended with Marsanne in the Rhone and Chardonnay in other areas. It does well with barrel fermentation and oak aging, being not as overtly fruity as some types and with notes of wildflowers or herbal tea.

- **Aneis**: This variety is grown in the Piedmont region of northwestern Italy, and traditionally yields a soft wine that matures early and has a slightly herbaceous aroma with almond flavors. It can also have a tropical fruit spicy flavor, and it is typically made with a dry finish.

- **Macabeo**: This varietal is grown mostly in northern Spain in Rioja and Languedoc. it is frequently blended with Malvasia and Garnacha Blanca (Grenache Blanc). It is also increasingly blended with Sauvignon Blanc and Chardonnay, and Cava sparkling wine. It has notable nose and mouth characteristics that include high oak character, freshness, and light fruit notes. It has a neutral floral character with medium-low acidity.

Red Grape Variety Characters

- **Cabernet Sauvignon**: This produces diverse, complex characters with typical flavors of black olives, black currant, blackberry, black plum and notes of chocolate, coffee, and spice. It has many nuances depending on the winemaking process. Warm fermentation enhances its flavors and extracts for tannin which gives the wine more body. Oak adds burned flavors and spiciness. Some of these varieties have more herbal, brambly, and spicy flavors with supple, savory characters. As it matures, this wine takes on more prune, stew fruit characters that adds more complexity. Other typical characters are mint and licorice.

- **Cabernet Franc**: The typical character for this variety is blackberry fruit with hints of raspberry. It is also herbal, peppery, and somewhat aromatic, and it is considered more approachable than the Cabernet Sauvignon.
- **Merlot**: The typical varietal characters associated with this grape are plum, leathery, fruitcake, gamey, and meaty. It is also occasionally described as black currant, plum, spice, and coffee. It is frequently blended with Bordeaux, because this grape is softer and doesn't have as stringent tannins.
- **Malbec**: This is frequently blended with other Bordeaux reds to add color, and it also adds rich, sweet, fruit flavors. Other characters include plum, spicy, and at times, slightly earthy.
- **Syrah**: The typical character of this varietal includes raspberry, blackberry, licorice, black pepper, plum, spice, and prunes. Additionally, maturation can add earthy notes that increase complexity and interest.
- **Pinot Noir**: The common characters for this grape varietal include strawberry, cherry, plum, raspberry, mushrooms, beetroot, and earthiness. It is also commonly described as straw, spicy, and nutty.
- **Zinfandel**: This varietal exhibits a dark-purple hue with characters of strawberry, plum, raisin, spice, leather, and tar. It is also commonly

described as chewy, spicy, and peppery. The color is deep red, bordering on black, and the intensity of flavors varies, but the basic Zinfandel flavor is similar.

- **Sangiovese**: The flavor characters of this grape include fruity with a moderate to high level of acidity and a medium-body that ranges from firm and elegant to assertive and robust. The finish can tend toward bitterness, and the aroma is not assertive but can include notes of strawberry, blueberry, floral, violet, or plum.

- **Carmenere**: This varietal produces a deep, red color and has aromas typical of red fruits, spices, and berries. The tannins are gentler and softer than a Cabernet Sauvignon, and the wine is medium-bodied. It is mostly used as a blending grape, but there are some vintners who bottle the pure varietal, which typically has a cherry character with smoky, spicy, and earthy notes. The taste can also remind you of dark chocolate, tobacco, and leather. The wine is best consumed when young.

- **Mourvedre**: This is frequently used in blends to boost their color and tannin level. The unblended wine has a deep-color, is quite tannic, moderately alcoholic, generally spice, and often gamey when young. Other characters include cinnamon, black pepper, thyme, and violet.

- **Nebbiolo**: Nebbiolo wines are typically dark, tart, tannic, and alcoholic with aromas of cherries, violets, roses, black licorice, truffles. They also have rich, chewy, deep, and long-lasting flavors that include mint, strawberry, and tar. It harmonizes best with rich, strong-flavored meats and stews as well as dry, aged cheeses that are too strong for other wines.

- **Tempranillo**: This wine is typically described as savory rather than sweet. The aromas include hints of leather, fresh tobacco leaves, and sappy, fresh vegetals. These wines are ruby red in color with tastes of berries, plum, vanilla, and herbs. While Tempranillo is frequently blended, it often makes up as much as 90 percent of the blend. It is low in acidity and sugar content, and most commonly blended with Grenache, Carignan, Graciano, Merlot, and Cabernet Sauvignon.
- **Montepulciano**: This varietal has sweet tannins and a jammy, soft flavor. It is a widely grown grape in Italy, the best known varieties of which are Montepulciano d'Abruzzo and Rosso Conero.
- **Petit Verdot**: This is known as the "small green" variety because it tends to ripen late. It is frequently used in Bordeaux style red blends, but it is declining in popularity because of its unpredictable maturation that often results in the loss of the entire crop. In the warmer climates of the New World, it is more reliable and commonly used in blends to strengthen the acidity and tannins. It also adds shades of dark purple color. It has distinctive flavors of blackberries along with aromas of banana and pencil shavings when young. When mature, it has notes of violets and leather.

WELL, NOW THAT YOU'RE CAUGHT UP ON THE terminology and characters of the common grape varietals, why not take a swirl and a swallow of your favorite wine and describe its character with your newly learned vocabulary?

Before you know it, you'll be describing wines just like the pros!

Chapter Summary

In this chapter, we've examined the character of the grape. We've specifically covered the following topics:

- What is meant by character;
- The terminology of the characters;
- The typical characteristics of the main grape varietals.

In the next chapter, we'll look at the fabulous five: red wine, white wine, fortified wine, sparkling wine, and dessert wine.

CHAPTER FOUR: THE FABULOUS FIVE: RED, WHITE, FORTIFIED, SPARKLING, AND DESSERT

Now that you're becoming an expert on the wine varietals, let's take a look at the categories of wine, specifically, these fabulous five: red, white, fortified, sparkling, and dessert. Rosé is often added as an additional category, and there are also subdivisions within these categories. But, let's begin with the basic categories and then we can look a little more at other divisions.

Red Wines

These are produced from what the industry calls black grapes, and though some are almost black, more are shades of red or blue. Red wines are frequently described as ruby, purple, gamet, or tawny in color. The color is the result of the contact between the grape skin and the juice. The main red wine types include the following:

- Cabernet Sauvignon, best paired with fatty, salty foods;
- Merlot, which is a more versatile wine and can be paired with vegetable-based dishes and tomato-based pastas;
- Malbec, which is best paired with sweet and spicy foods;
- Pinot Noir, which is ideally paired with a barbecue-glazed salmon;

- Syrah/Shiraz, which goes well with spicy foods;
- Zinfandel, which goes well with foods that have tart sauces and cheese;
- Sangiovese, which goes well with Italian foods and gamey meats.

White Wines

White wines are not actually white, but rather shades of straw, yellow, or gold, and sometimes, they are almost clear. They're made with white grapes, which also aren't white, but rather shades of green or grey. They can also be made, however, from red grapes, which are not really red, but called black grapes instead. As you can see, you need a few glasses of wine to understand the color scheme in this industry. The main white wine types include the following:

- Chardonnay, which pairs well with creamy dishes and those containing umami;
- Sauvignon Blanc, which pairs well with cheese dishes, and those with more mineral characters also go well with seafood;
- Moscato, which goes well with spicy food;
- Pinot Grigio, which goes well with creamy pasta dishes;
- Gewurztraminer, which goes well with spicy Asian foods;
- Riesling, which goes well with spicy Indian dishes;
- Viognier, which goes well with salads and some seafoods like shrimp.

Fortified Wines

Fortified wines are called by this name because they have brandy or other kinds of spirits added to the wine during the fermentation process. That actually stops the fermentation and leaves the wine sweet and higher in alcohol content than achieved with the standard grape fermentation. Fortified wines like Port, Sherry, and Madeira were specifically developed to survive long sea voyages. Other fortified wines, like late-harvest Riesling and Sauternes, are frequently served as dessert wines, and the most popular Catholic communion wine, Angelica, is a fortified wine. The main fortified wine types include the following:

- Madeira, made in Portugal on the island of the same name;
- Marsala, an Italian specialty from the southern region;
- Port Wine, which is now produced throughout the world;
- Sherry, produced in southern Spain;
- Vermouth, which is better known as an ingredient in a martini, but it's also a nice aperitif that is either dry or sweet.

Sparkling Wines

Sparkling wines are made from every type of grape, but are distinguished from each other in the fermentation process. The process produces carbon dioxide, but in still wines that CO_2 escapes as the wine matures in barrels. The difference with a sparkling wine is that the CO_2 is held in the wine, thereby producing the bubbles. The main kinds of sparkling wines include the following:

- Champagne, which is the best known of sparkling wines. It is made from three grapes: Chardonnay, Pinot Noir, and Pinot Meunier, and it is only Champagne when the grapes are grown and the wine is made in Champagne, France;
- New World Sparkling Wine, for which the United States is at the forefront in crafting a range of sparkling wine options, though often with an Old World flair;
- Italian Prosecco, which is light, white, and ultra-fresh. It is produced in Veneto in northeast Italy south of Venice.
- Spanish Cava, which is made in the traditional method of Champagne that includes a second, bubble-trapping fermentation process, which takes place in the bottle instead of a tank.

DESSERT WINES

Dessert wines are high in sugar, and are produced from grapes that are harvested very late, even after a frost in the case of ice wines, for example. They can also be made by drying grapes on straw mats to turn them into raisins, as is done with Amarone. Dessert wines do not have added spirits, although some fortified wines are used as dessert wines. The main types of dessert wines are as follows:

- Sparkling dessert wines, which use sweeter smelling grape varieties to trick the brain into thinking the wine is sweeter than it is. Words to look for on the label include demi-sec (off-dry in French), amabile (slightly sweet in Italian), semi-secco (off-dry in Italian), doux (sweet in French),

dolce/dulce (sweet in Italian/Spanish), moelleux
(sweet for some French wines);

- Lightly sweet dessert wines, which are
  refreshingly sweet and perfect for a warm
  afternoon and pair well with spicy foods. They
  are best enjoyed close to the vintage date. A few
  examples include Gewurztraminer, Riesling,
  Muller-Thurgau, Chenin Blanc, and Viognier.
- Richly sweet dessert wines, which are made with
  the highest quality grapes in an unfortified style.
  These wines can age more than 50 years since the
  sweetness and acidity preserve their fresh flavor.
  Some examples include Tokaji from Hungary,
  Constantia from South Africa, and Sauternes
  from France.
- Late harvest dessert wines, which are sweeter
  since the grapes hang on the vine longer and
  become more raisinated. Examples include late
  harvest dessert wines made from Chenin Blanc,
  Semillon, and Riesling grapes.
- Noble rot, which are wines affected by the spore,
  Botrytis cinerea which eats fruits and vegetables. It
  sounds bad, but it adds flavors of ginger, saffron,
  and honey to sweet wines. Examples of noble rot
  dessert wines include Tokaji, Sauternais, and
  Auslese.
- Straw mat dessert wines, which are where the
  grapes are allowed to dry out on a straw mat and
  raisinate prior to winemaking. Examples include
  the Italian Vin Santo, Italian Passito, and Samos,
  a Greek wine made from Muscat grapes.
- Ice wine (Eiswein) which is extremely rare
  because it occurs only in those bizarre years where

a vineyard freezes, and it must be harvested while the grapes are still frozen. Canada is the largest ice wine producer in the world, but it is also produced in the cooler regions of Germany, Austria, and Switzerland. Examples include Riesling and Cabernet Franc.

- Sweet red wines, which are on the decline, but there are some that are still worth trying, most of which are from Italy using esoteric grapes. Examples include Lambrusco, Brachetto d'Acqui, and Schiava.

And a Few More Categories...

Rosé: Rosé wines fall in between reds and whites, and are frequently categorized as red. They are produced sometimes by having brief contact with the skins of black or red grapes in a short fermentation time of between 12 and 36 hours. Other times, they are made by blending red and white wines together. The flavors range from dry to sweet with pale to dark pink colors and a lower level of tannin. They go well with light flavor dishes such as fish, poultry, or fruit.

Brandy: Brandy in general refers to liquors distilled from fruits like pears, cherries, and plums, but the most popular after-dinner beverage refers to distilled grape juice. It is made from a still wine that uses early grapes, and the distillation process turns wine into brandy as it increases the alcohol content. After distillation, the beverage is aged, which is vital to develop a good quality. Brandy is typically aged in oak barrels to help develop the color. Cognac is the world's most famous brandy, and it is made only in the city of Cognac in the southwest of France.

You're now caught up on the categories of wine and some of the more common food pairings. it's time to try some of those categories you don't typically drink, perhaps a good fortified wine or a nice dessert wine. Or maybe, you're not a lover of white wines, but now that you know a little more about them, you might find some that better suit your style.

Chapter Summary

In this chapter, we've discussed the fabulous five categories of wine and a few extra categories as well. Specifically, we've discussed the following topics:

- Red and white wines;
- Fortified wines;
- Sparkling wines;

- Dessert wines;
- Rosé and Brandy.

In the next chapter, you'll discover how to improve your palate.

CHAPTER FIVE: IMPROVING YOUR PALATE

Now we're getting down to the good stuff – tasting the wine and improving your palate. You've probably heard a sommelier talk about wine using phrases like, "The nose carries notes of crushed strawberries, fig, and fresh roses," and you might have thought to yourself, "I would never be able to detect that." The reality is, however, that you can train your palate to pick out those delicate flavors and aromas. And, the best part is, it takes practice! That means drinking more wine. It's a hard job, but someone's gotta do it, right?

Some people are simply born with taste buds that experience flavor at a heightened intensity, but most people have to develop their palate through persistent work. When you're talking about your palate, you're really talking about a close relationship between your sense of smell and your taste buds. A big part of tasting is actually smelling. You can even test that by chewing on a piece of really stinky cheese with your nose pinched shut, then let your nose open and notice how different the cheese tastes when you're including smell.

So, how can you improve your palate to detect the

nuances of flavors and smells in most wines? The good news is that there are some concrete ways to improve your palate, and they're very enjoyable. Here are some of the tips that come from winemakers, sommeliers, and industry pros for helping to improve your tasting skills:

Start From Where You Are

There's no minimum level of experience or ability required. Don't judge yourself as too green. Anyone can improve their palate. It might take a year or even more, but you can develop your palate, and it will change your relationship with wine and food. Some people even claim it was the best thing they could have done for their health. Developing your palate can result in cravings for healthy food.

The Nose Knows

YOU WANT TO BE ABLE TO SMELL THE AROMAS IN THE wine, but to do this, you'll have to release those aromas by introducing oxygen to the wine juice. That's why you swirl the glass before sniffing it. To do this, the glass should not be too full. Place it on the table and pinch the stem between your thumb, index, and middle fingers. Begin to move the glass in a circle, and hold it up to get your nose inside the glass. This should allow you to experience the bouquet much more intensely. Close your eyes as you inhale. You don't have to just do this wine either; the next time you're about to eat something, smell it first. Practice can help train your brain to separate out aromas into distinct parts. Pretty soon, you'll be able to smell raspberries or blackberries where other people just smell something vinous.

Another thing you can do to educate your palate with respect to aroma is go to the produce section of the grocery store, and instead of smelling the roses, smell the fruits, vegetables, and herbs. This will help you to identify particular aromas in your wine. Your olfactory system is tied very strongly to your memory, and once you have the memory of those smells, you'll be better able to identify them in other places. Spice shops are another potential training ground too. Spices are the building blocks of food, and you can really train your nose by smelling these in their more accessible state. It might also be a good idea to buy what is called an "essences collection" that includes 24 vials of scents commonly found in wine. This allows the pros in the wine industry as well as perfumers and coffee roasters to identify individual olfactory notes with precision.

Aspiration

This is an absolutely essential skill to educate your palate for wine tasting. To do it, you basically have to slow down, take a sip of wine and roll it over your tongue while at the same time sucking air into it. This brings in oxygen to the sip which, in turn, releases more of the wine's flavors. That will allow you to notice more of the characters in the wine, such as oakiness or acidity. While doing this, you'll have to really focus on the wine in your mouth and leave it there for a relatively long time. Some wine experts advise chewing it around. You might inhale a little wine the first few times you do this, but keep practicing and you will get the hang of it.

Use Your Words

The pros always carry around a notebook with them to jot down the various aromas and flavors they're experiencing as they're tasting wines, and you should do the same thing. It's easy to do at home or in a restaurant, and over time, you'll begin to be able to identify the distinct characters of wine and discuss them with confidence. It will also help you start learning and using the vocabulary words used in the industry. Plus, by tasting and describing the wine at the same time, you'll enhance your memory for both the flavors and the language used to describe them.

Refine Your Vocabulary

There's no wrong way to describe wine, but there are some words that can be misleading. For example, the word sweet is frequently used incorrectly to describe fruitiness or oakiness. Wine will be dry and not sweet unless it has some residual sugar like, for example, dessert wines. This is because the process of creating a dessert wine never ferments the juice from the grape dry. To use the term 'sweet' correctly, it really means that the wine is juicy, low in acidity, and perhaps oaky, something some experts call fruit-forward.

When you're verbally or in written form describing wine, you want to consider the wine's body, the acidity level, the tannins, the floral components, and the alcohol level. To experience these flavors in another setting so you can recognize their taste in wine, try sipping lemon juice for acidity, overly steeped tea for tannin, and for body, taste the difference between skim milk, whole milk, and heavy cream. For alcohol, take a shot of tequila to experience that. These are great ways to help you detect those flavors in wine. Once you've got the tastes down, now you can look for them in wine and see if you can pick out the different components. You can even rate them on a scale of low-high for the wine.

Drink!

This is the easiest, and most enjoyable, method to train your palate. To really be able to pick out the flavor and aroma differences, you need to be tasting wine as frequently as possible. Just like any other skill, you need practice, and nothing can substitute for popping that cork. As you practice, you'll be building a palatal memory, and you'll begin to be able to discern ever more subtle tastes and aromas in the wines you taste. To practice properly, though, it's important to follow the tips described above – swirl the glass, aspirate, and jot down your experience of the wine. It can also help to learn more about the wine you're tasting. Where is it from? What technique was used in making it? As you learn to associate the tastes and aromas you're experiencing with the different winemaking regions, you'll start associating certain flavors and aromas with various regions of the world and different wine styles.

In this regard, it can help to establish a daily practice of tasting. Dedicate a few hours daily or weekly to sampling various wines with some good friends. Choose a few bottles from a particular region of the world, producer, or grape varieties to sample and discuss. As you do this again and again, your palate will become more sophisticated, the flavors will become more familiar, and you will begin to develop your wine instinct and intuition. You can even look at it as a kind of mindfulness practice. That is, after all, what you're doing – being mindful of the wine in your mouth. You and your friends can learn the distinctive flavors of wines from different regions together. It will be fun and educational.

Compare and Contrast

While you're sampling various wines, you'll want to compare and contrast wines at the same time. Try sampling two semi-related bottles – something like a bottle of Champagne and one of Prosecco. Then, compare the two for subtle flavors and aromas, body, acidity, and tannins. In this way, you'll also be able to discover the subtleties of your own preferences. By sampling them at the same time, you'll see what you do like about one versus the other and vice versa. You also want to do vertical comparisons. That's where you taste the same style of wine from different years. That will help you to understand how the weather and other variables affect the different vintages. You'll also learn whether you prefer wines from hotter versus cooler regions.

Blind Tasting

This refers to tasting a wine that you don't have any information about, so you won't have any expectations regarding its flavors and aromas. In the wine industry, it's common for professionals to be presented with wines wrapped in brown paper bags or aluminum foil. That way, they don't know where the wine came from or even what it cost. This will allow you to evaluate the wine without any kind of prejudice, and it's fun too.

No matter the level of your experience, training your palate for tasting wine is something that will teach you as much about yourself as about the wine. Wine is, after all, meant to be enjoyed, not simply sampled. As you train your palate, you'll find you are enjoying the wine more, because you'll be distinguishing the subtle flavors and truly savoring the entire experience. Your palate and your wine experience will be better because of your new-found wine-tasting talent.

CHAPTER SUMMARY

In this chapter, we've discussed how to improve your palate for the wine tasting experience. Specifically, we've discussed the following topics:

- Starting from your baseline and improving your palate;
- The importance of the smell in the wine tasting experience;
- How to release the subtle aromas of wine;
- Aspiration and proper tasting techniques;
- Using produce markets and spice stores to train your palate and your brain;
- Experience is key, so drink up!

In the next chapter, you'll learn about the etiquette of wine tasting.

CHAPTER SIX: WINE TASTING ETIQUETTE – THE DO'S AND DON'TS

Now that you're learning much more about the flavors and aromas of your favorite wines, you'll likely want to visit a winery or two and have a formal tasting experience. Wine tasting events are fun ways to sample great wines and pass some time with good friends. You can also try the new wines without having to buy a bottle if you don't like them. But, there is a certain etiquette at a wine tasting event, and it's helpful to know all about the dos and don'ts, so let's dive right in.

THE DOS

There are a number of things you should do at a wine tasting event that you might not do in other situations. And, there are some things you might not think about, so knowing what to do will help you seem like you've been doing this all your life.

- **Have a plan**: If you're walking around tasting a lot of wines, the experience can become overwhelming very quickly. That's even true for professionals. So, you want to have a plan of attack. You might, for example, give yourself a theme for the tasting event. You might start with white wines from a particular region that were made with a specific grape variety. Taste five or six of those and then make note of the differences. By planning a theme, you can learn much more from the event, and not have to be carried out of the place!

- **Take notes**: Taking notes will help you remember the wines you liked and the ones you didn't. You might use your new vocabulary or your own language to describe them, and then, give them a score from one to ten based on how much you liked the wine. As you get more comfortable with vocabulary used to describe wine, you'll find you're using it more often as well. Be sure to bring a pen and paper just in case the winery doesn't provide them.

- **Try something new**: Be sure to take advantage of the wine tasting event to try something new. If you find something you really like, take note of the region and grape variety that produced it. While doing this, it is important to let go of any misconceptions you might have about wines you think you won't like. There will be some you won't like, but there may be one that becomes your new favorite. Don't limit your experience by assuming you will or won't like a particular variety.

- **Ask questions**: Good wine tasting hosts are approachable and love to get questions. It's their job to know the details, so take advantage of their presence. Don't be afraid to ask about the wines you like; find out their background, the grape variety, the region, the winemaking method, and as much as you can about the different samples. By filling in the context, you'll appreciate the wine even more. There are no stupid questions either, so ask whatever you want to know.

- **Cleanse your palate**: You do this by taking a sip

of water between tastings, and use it also to swill your glass. Also, you might be offered crackers or other snacks during your tasting. These are meant to be a substitute for lunch; they're there to help cleanse your palate as well. These will help you get the taste of the wine you just tasted out of your mouth before you move on to the next wine. You want a clean palate to fully appreciate its flavors and aromas.

- **Spit**: This is one of those things you don't do at a lot of places and events, but it's okay with wine tasting. It just gets better and better, doesn't it? All joking aside, it's important to spit sometimes or you'll end up being that horrible drunk at the wine tasting, and you don't want to be that person. Certainly, you'll swallow some – and you can swallow all you want – but if you want to remember the experience you had and not have to be embarrassed to return to the winery, you want to practice some spitting. That will help you keep tabs on how much you've consumed.

- **Dump**: If you haven't finished a glass of wine and it's time to move on to a new sample, don't be afraid to dump out the excess. It is not considered rude, but if you just can't bring yourself to do it, ask for the new wine to be poured into a separate glass.

- **Tip if it's indicated**: Many times, tasting room staff receive a commission for sales, but each business is structured differently. If there is a tip jar or your bill includes a line for gratuity, take that as an indication that the staff is depending, to some extent, on tips for their wages.

THE DON'TS

Now that you've got your list of Dos at a wine-tasting event, let's look at the don'ts.

- **Don't be afraid to respectfully give your opinion**: Wine tasting is a subjective experience. Only you can say if you like a particular variety or not, and if you don't, that's not wrong. Don't be afraid to share your honest opinion with your friends and other guests, including the host. Once the host knows the kinds of wines you like, they'll likely match your taste with similar wines. Just don't be rude as you do this. Nobody likes an obnoxious wine taster!
- **Don't guzzle**: The point of the wine tasting experience is to savor both the wine and the experience. So, don't just throw back glass after glass of wine; savor it to the fullest by following these four easy steps:
- Look – check out the color and the clarity. Don't just describe it as red, say what kind of red it is – ruby, plum, maroon, purple, brown, or any other version of red out there. Then, check out the clarity. Is it watery or dark, clear or cloudy?
- Swirl – as you swirl your glass, droplets of wine will cling to the inside of the glass, and the more that do, the higher the alcohol content. Also, since swirling introduces oxygen to the wine and releases the aromas, this is a good opportunity to get your first whiff of the wine.
- Smell – once you've finished swirling, bring the glass to your nose for your second impression as

you take in the aroma. Is it a fruity and what
kind – dark black or crunchy red? What don't
you smell? The answer to that question can help
you identify what you do smell.

- Sip and Savor – now it's time to taste. Sip rather
  than gulp, and let the wine roll around in your
  mouth. Aspirate and analyze the texture. Breathe
  out after swallowing to see how long the flavor
  lasts. If it disappears quickly, the finish is short; if
  it linger, the finish is long. A long finish is,
  generally speaking, a sign of good quality.

- **Don't wear perfume or aftershave – nothing
  scented**: Unless you want to annoy the people
  around you, you shouldn't wear anything scented.
  It identifies you as an amateur and interferes with
  the wine tasting experience of those around you.
  You can always bring some in a bag and put it on
  after the event if you feel you need it, but go
  without while tasting.

- **Don't hold the bowl**: Your wine glass should be
  held by the stem, not the bowl. If you hold it by
  the bowl, you'll get your grubby fingerprints all
  over the glass, but more importantly, you'll affect
  the temperature of the wine which will change
  your tasting experience. It's also a sure-fire way to
  get under the skin of the wine snobs around you.

- **Don't go on an empty stomach**: You definitely
  want to have something to eat before going on a
  wine tasting event. The small sips add up quickly,
  and without something solid in your stomach,
  you might spend more time in the bathroom
  than the tasting room.

- **Don't hog the bar**: A lot of wine tasting rooms
  that have standing bars get crowded, so if that's

the case, take a step back from the bar when you've got your sample. That will allow others to get theirs, and you can return to the bar when you're ready for your next pour.
- **Don't wear white**: You will get wine on whatever you're wearing, so make sure it's not white and it's not your Sunday best.

These tips will help you, and those around you, enjoy the wine tasting experience. You'll get to taste many different wines and discover new favorites as well as better train your palate. And, you'll look like a pro while you do. So, take the time to truly savor your next wine tasting experience now that you know the etiquette.

CHAPTER SUMMARY

In this chapter, we've discussed the dos and don'ts of the wine tasting event. Specifically, we've covered the following topics:

- The proper etiquette regarding what you should do at a wine tasting event;
- Spit, dump, and tip are among the most important dos at a wine tasting event;
- Cleanse, savor, ask questions, and take notes are also helpful dos;
- Guzzle, hold the bowl, hog the bar, or wear white are among the most important don'ts;
- Don't wear perfume, be afraid to ask questions, or go on an empty stomach are other helpful don'ts.

In the next chapter, you will learn how to choose a bottle.

CHAPTER SEVEN: CHOOSING THE BOTTLE

To choose the proper bottle of wine, it's important to consider the occasion, flavor preferences, labels, and price points. The combination of these factors is different for every person, but there are some tips that can help with selecting a good bottle of wine. So, sit back, take a moment to savor that glass of wine you're sipping, and let's talk about choices.

NEWBIES – START WITH WHITE OR ROSÉ. THE WINES YOU enjoy over time, like your food preferences, will mature and change. But, a study by Sonoma State University found that most people whose first experience with wine is a sweet white or rosé will later come to love dry reds or wines that have more distinctive flavors. Having an early distaste for the drier wines or those higher in tannins might be due to their unique flavors and sharp bitterness. By starting with lighter-bodied wines, most people will then develop a taste for the more unique flavors.

WHAT OTHER FLAVORS DO YOU ENJOY? FLAVORS THAT you like in other foods and drinks can indicate the types of wines you might like. If you have a sweet tooth, for example, you'll likely enjoy sweeter wines. If you prefer something bitter like black coffee, that might mean a more acidic wine is your cup of tea (pun intended). Here are two questions to start with for discovering your taste preferences:

1. ***Do you prefer grapefruit juice or apple juice?*** Those who like grapefruit juice would likely prefer a dry, white wine, while those who like apple juice probably prefer a sweet, white wine.
2. ***Do you prefer a latte or black coffee?*** Those who prefer black coffee will likely prefer an Old World wine, one that comes from the locations where winemaking first began, like France, Italy, or Spain. If your preference is for a latte, it's likely you'll prefer a New World Wine, such as something from the United States, Argentina, or Chile.

WHAT'S THE OCCASION? WILL THIS WINE BOTTLE BE just for you or are you sharing? Are you pairing it with a specific meal? The occasion will influence how you choose a wine. Here are some questions to ask yourself when you're out shopping:

- ***Do you want a crowd-pleaser?*** If you're wanting to please your family and friends as opposed to pairing the wine with a food, you can simply pick a bottle of white and a bottle of red. Having one of each will be sure to please several palates, and you can choose wines that are closer to the middle on the spectrum of sweetness, acidity, and body. Those kinds of balanced, moderate flavors are likely to appeal to more of your guests.
- ***Are you pairing with a meal?*** If your objective is

to pair the wine with food, then the general rule
is white wines for lighter dishes such as chicken
and fish, and red wines for heavier dishes such as
beef and lamb. But, see below for more details.

- ***Are you mixing the wine or drinking it solo?*** If,
for example, you're mixing the wine into another
cocktail or summer sangria, then the subtle
flavors of the wines are not as important. If you're
using it for a cooking recipe, the flavors will
blend into the sauce or meat and accent those.
For these occasions, a less expensive bottle of
wine will work fine, but if you're planning on
drinking the wine on its own, you'll want to be
more critical as you select for your favorite flavor
notes.

- ***Do you know what you're buying?*** Read the
label and understand what you're reading. It's
common for clever labels to sway people into
buying a wine that might not really be the best
choice for them. That's why it's critical to read
the label and understand what it means. The
first thing to look for are details about the
region, valley, and grapes. The more
information, generally, the better. The next thing
to look for is the winery name, grape variety,
year of harvest, the region where the grapes were
grown, the alcohol percentage, and the
description, the latter of which is usually on the
back of the label. You now have a better
understanding of the basic characteristics of
sweetness, acidity, tannin, body, and alcohol,
and the language used to describe them, so that
will help you decipher the description of these as
wella s the aromas and flavors listed. If you like

the flavors in the descriptions, it's probably a wine you'll like.

- **_Look for "second-label" wines._** When grapes are harvested, the best, fully mature grapes are used for the primary batch of wine, called the "first label." These frequently have two qualities in common: 1) they are available in limited quantities, and 2) they are expensive. You might want to pay that price; however, if you're just starting out, the price tag can be tough to justify if you're not sure about what you're buying. That's why second-label wines can be a good alternative. Second-label wines are those made with grapes that might not be as mature or polished for the first label. These go through the same process of winemaking that is nearly identical to the first label, but it is then sold under a different name. Hence, the term second label. The wine is from the same expert vineyard, so you get the same high-quality wine, but it costs you much less than the first label wine would. If you're familiar with some of the big-name wineries, you will probably be able to spot a second label since they often incorporate some part of their winery name. Also, a bit of research will point you in the right direction to find a good second label wine to try.
- **_Age is just a number._** The perception is that the older the wine, the better. Some wines do taste better with age, but others are better shortly after bottling. In fact, most wines are not meant to be aged and should be consumed within five years of purchasing them. But, it really depends on the wine. Also, proper aging of wine is dependent on several factors, including the region it comes

from, the amounts of tannings, the sugars, and the acids. Generally speaking, aging is more important for red wines than it is for white wines, but any wine you purchase in a store should be ready for drinking.

- ***Don't go by price***. A wine that is on sale is not indicative of its quality. It might be on sale because it's been in the store's inventory for a while or it's not in season, but neither has anything to do with quality. Also, choosing an expensive wine with the thought that it will be of higher quality will only end up disappointing you. Always go by the flavors and characters you prefer rather than the price, which should only be a secondary consideration.
- **Don't discount bottles with screw caps**. Many people think bottles with screw caps mean the wine is low quality, but that's not necessarily true. The caps were designed for bottles of wine that are meant to be consumed within the same year of bottling for reasons of freshness and acidity. Screwcap bottles can be much more convenient

than a cork, particularly for occasions where you might not have an opener handy, like a picnic, and it's easier to pack them up and take them home. So, don't be afraid to sample those; they often hold great tasting wine.

- *Keep track of the wines you've sampled*. It's helpful to make an inventory of sorts for the wines you've sampled. Make note of the name, region, and variety of grapes. There are even apps that will allow you to record this information. Since choosing a good wine is all about what you prefer, if you keep track of what you've sampled and what you thought of it, you'll be better at picking out the right wine for you. If you use an app, you'll have the information handy when you're at the store, so you can make better choices. If you find you consistently like wine from a particular region, you can sample varieties from that location, or if it's a particular grape variety you prefer, you can shop around for wines from that grape. By keeping track of the information, you'll always be able to choose the right wine for you.

- *Don't forget to try something new every now and again*. Your wine notes will help you keep track of your taste preferences, but branch out once in a while. As you continue to try new wines, your tastes may change over time, and you don't want to miss out on your new favorite wine.

Choosing a Wine for Dinner

WHILE THE TIPS ABOVE WORK FOR SEVERAL SITUATIONS, there are some specific things to think about when you're choosing a wine to pair with a meal. In this case, you want the flavors to enhance one another, and it is equally true that a good wine can go unnoticed if it is paired with the wrong food. To begin, it's important to review the basic wine characters of sweetness, acidity, tannin, body, and alcohol since you will be using these for pairing purposes.

The goal of choosing a wine to go with your meal is to either complement the food flavors or offer a contrast to the food flavors. If you have paired the wine and meal well, you will create a burst of flavor from both the dining and drinking experience. Here are a few things to remember:

- **Acid food typically requires an acid wine**.
  Meals that include citrus fruits or fish tend to be higher in acidity, and if you choose a low acidity wine, you'll likely be disappointed by the pairing,

because the acidity in the food will overpower the wine. So, remember to fight acid with acid!

- **Salty and sweet are a good pair**. Just like with food combinations of salty and sweet, the same is true for a choice of wine. If the meal is a salty one, a sweet wine will help cut the saltiness, and the sweet flavor of the wine will also be highlighted.

- **Fatty foods call for a bitter, high acidity, or high alcohol content wine**. If the dish you've having is fatty, there are a couple of choices for your wine pairing. The first is a bitter wine. This is seen in the classic combination of steak and a bitter, red wine. The second is to match the meal with a high-acidity wine as with a white wine butter sauce like beurre blanc. The acidity cuts through the fat. Another example of this is pairing a rich, fatty cheesecake with a high acidity wine. It creates wonderful flavor sensations, and you get those same sensations with a wine that has a higher alcohol content.

- **Foods and wines from the same region can make great pairs**. It makes sense that foods and wines from the same region would pair well, and they usually do. So, for example, if you're eating an Italian dish, you might select a fine Italian wine with complementary characteristics. The pairs don't always work, but they usually do.

Now that you have an idea of the general characteristics to look for when pairing wines with your meals, let's look at some specific wines, their characteristics, and the best foods to pair them with:

- **Riesling**: This light to medium-bodied white wine has lots of fruit flavors, is moderately sweet, and high in acidity. It pairs well with the following foods: chicken, pork, duck, turkey, cured meat, and several Thai, Indian, Moroccan, Vietnamese, and German meals.
- **Pinot Gris**: This light-bodied white wine has a medium-level of acidity and subtle, sweet fruit and floral flavors. It pairs well with salads, poached fish, and light or mild cheeses.
- **Sauvignon Blanc**: This light to medium-bodied white wine has lots of citrus fruit flavors, and it is high in acidity. It pairs well with the following dishes: fish, chicken, pork, veal, herb-crusted or nutty cheeses, and many Mexican, Vietnamese, and French meals.
- **Chardonnay**: This medium to full-bodied white wine has many yellow fruit flavors and a medium level of acidity. It pairs well with shrimp, crab, lobster, chicken, pork, mushrooms, cream sauces, soft or nutty cheeses, and several French dishes.
- **Pinot Noir**: This light-bodied, red wine has fewer tannins and high levels of acidity with red fruit flavors. It pairs well with the following foods: chicken, pork, veal, duck, cured meats, soft or nutty cheeses, cream sauces, and several French and German dishes.
- **Zinfandel**: This medium to full-bodied, red wine has higher levels of fruit flavors and a lower level of acidity. It pairs well with the following foods: chicken, pork, cured meat, lamb, beef, barbecue, and several Italian, American, Chinese, Indian, and Thai dishes.
- **Syrah**: This full-bodied, red wine has moderate

levels of tannins and higher fruits flavors and acidity. It pairs well with the following foods: beef, lamb, smoked meats, white cheddar cheese, and several Mediterranean, American, and French dishes.

- **Cabernet Sauvignon**: This full-bodied, red wine usually has high levels of tannins and alcohol. It pairs well with the following foods: lamb, beef, smoked meats, aged cheddar cheese, and several French and American meals.

Now, you're up to speed on choosing the best bottle of wine for any occasion. You know what pairs well with different kinds of foods as well as what to do when you are choosing for the wine itself rather than pairing it with a meal. Why not treat your friends and family to a good bottle of wine tonight!

CHAPTER SUMMARY

In this chapter, we've covered how to choose the right bottle of wine for almost any occasion. Specifically, we've covered the following topics:

- How to choose a wine you will like;
- How your food preferences predict your wine preferences;
- How to choose wine for different occasions;
- The specifics of pairing a wine with a meal.

In the next chapter, we'll discuss the art of serving wine.

CHAPTER EIGHT: THE ART OF SERVING WINE

Now that you know how to choose the best wine for different occasions, how to sample wine, and how to describe wine, you need to know how to serve wine. There's more to it than simply opening a bottle and pouring. And, it's something that, when you know how to do it properly, you can make a festive occasion out of it. There are a few simple rules to think about so that you and your guests will enjoy every last drop.

Temperature: Just like with many different foods and drinks – think about soda, for example – temperature is an important factor when serving wine. The first rule is don't serve the wine warm, and that's whether it's a red or white wine. If they are served warm, you tend to only be able to perceive the dominating presence of alcohol in red wine or unpleasant acidity in white wine. When it tastes like that, you won't even want to finish the first glass. In general, white wines should be kept in the refrigerator. While they might not be the ideal temperature when they're opened, it will likely warm up to ideal quickly. You can also use an ice bucket to keep white wines cool while you're serving them. But, depending on the particular variety, you might need more ice or more water in the bucket. For example, barrel-aged Chardonnays like Vinya Gigi don't need as much ice, but other types of Chardonnay need more ice than water. By getting them more or less to the ideal temperature, you'll be able to appreciate the full complexity of the wine. Rosés should be treated similarly to white wine; use an ice bucket to keep it cooler so the temperature won't rise too much. For reds, forget about the idea of serving them at room temperature. Here's a guide for the best temperatures:

Serving temperatures:

- Light white and rosés should be served at 7 to 10 degrees celsius (44 to 50 degrees fahrenheit);
- Sparkling wines should be served at 6 to 8 degrees celsius (43 to 46 degrees fahrenheit);
- Barrel-aged whites and rosés should be served at 10 to 12 degrees celsius (50 to 54 degrees fahrenheit);
- Young reds should be served at 12 to 15 degrees celsius (54 to 59 degrees fahrenheit);
- Barrel-aged reds should be served at 17 to 18 degrees celsius (62.5 to 64.5 degrees fahrenheit);

If your wine isn't chilled, the best way to do that quickly is to fill a suitable container – any bucket will do – with ice, water, and a pinch of salt, and within minutes, you'll have a nice, cool bottle of wine.

Cutting the capsule or foil: This refers to cutting the foil around the bottleneck, and it is done either just above or just below the rim. Wine sommeliers will cut the foil below the rim. This developed as the tradition given that foils were previously made of lead. Additionally, cutting below the rim will reduce the number of stray drips when pouring. But, the foil cutters are typically designed to cut the top of the lip, and this is sometimes done when the wine is on display because it is more visually appealing.

Of Corkscrews and Corks

As far as the choice of a corkscrew, the decision is yours based on whichever one you find easiest to use. Some of the easier ones to use are those that use a lever arm to lift the cork out of the bottle. These are called the Waiter's Friend. Whichever one you use, however, you want to make sure you position the corkscrew slightly off-center so that the radial diameter of the 'worm' – that's the curlycue part of the wine opener – will be centered as it penetrates the cork. You also don't want to push the corkscrew all the way through the cork. By using the corkscrew in this manner, you'll prevent loose bits of cork from falling into the wine. Once you've removed the cork, you'll also want to clean inside of the bottleneck to make sure there aren't small pieces of cork left inside.

Once you've removed the cork, tradition holds, and most

wine experts agree, you should inspect the cork. That includes smelling it. The things you want to inspect about the cork include the following:

- Is the cork branded, and if so, is it from the correct winery and vintage that you bought? While it's unlikely in the modern world, the ritual began as a means to spot fraudulent bottles.
- The other thing you want to inspect is the integrity of the cork. You can look for any signs that something is not right, but this really means smelling it. Many people will tell you not to smell the cork, but the majority of experts will tell you that smelling the cork is a vital part of evaluating the wine bottle.

The reason you smell the cork is that there is a natural contaminant called *trichloroanisole*, also called TCA. This causes 'cork taint.' When people refer to a wine as being 'corked,' this is what they mean. What can happen if you don't smell the cork for signs of this is that about 15 to 30 minutes later, the taint will start to show. When it's subtle, it will simply mute the aromas and flavors of the wine, but when it's stronger, the wine will smell and taste like a damp, moldy basement. You're also looking for this when you sample the wine after a server pours it, so why not just taste it and skip smelling the cork?

The answer is that the most likely source of TCA is the cork itself, and so the odor will be concentrated in the cork, and it might not be as evident in the wine. Additionally, while it might be subtle at first, as the wine is exposed to oxygen, the taste becomes more prominent. If you don't sniff the cork, you might think the wine is fine until some 15 to

30 minutes later, and if you're at a restaurant, you're now in the awkward position of having to tell the server that, although you pronounced the wine sound, you now realize it is corked. That's an uncomfortable situation and why smelling the cork can be your friend. While it's not 100 percent guaranteed that you'll detect TCA taint by smelling the cork, for most sommeliers, they're able to detect it about 90 percent of the time using this technique.

In addition to preventing an embarrassing situation at a restaurant, if you smell the cork in bottles you open at home, you'll prevent yourself from contaminating your glass with highly corked wine. You'll also educate yourself more about what good wine should smell like and what it should not smell like. The smell of a tainted cork will be like wet cardboard. The smell might be faint or strong, and it will get worse from there. You'll likely be able to pick up obvious examples right away, but over time, you'll get better at detecting subtler faults.

Decanting, Aerating, and Filtering

We've talked in several places about oxygenating the wine and what that does. It brings out the aromas and intensifies the wine's flavor. But, decanting is different from aerating. The purpose of decanting is to remove the sediments that have developed in the wine over time. Almost every red wine will taste better with decanting. The classic method that many people use is to pour the wine into a decanter or pitcher and let it sit for approximately 30 to 45 minutes.

DECANTING SHOULD BE DONE VERY CAREFULLY SO THAT you don't pour the sediments into the glass. A faster way to do this is to aerate the wine. This means that you pour it vigorously so that you oxygenate the wine as you pour. It's kind of like opening a window to let in some fresh air, and it will help to reduce unpleasant aromas that can be acquired, particularly in younger wines, when the wine is locked into the bottle. The wine can also be filtered using a fine metal sieve. This will further reduce the sediment in the wine, and it will reduce any particles suspended in the wine. There's nothing wrong with drinking those particles – they're completely harmless – but many people simply prefer to filter those out.

About the Glass

You might not think the glass has anything to do with

the wine taste, and what college student hasn't sipped wine from a plastic cup? But, the truth is that the proper glass will make any wine taste better. In fact, a 10th generation Austrian glassmaker named Georg Riedel proved it in 1986. He came out with a line of affordable machine-made crystal glass sets called Vinum. It includes different glass shapes for different types of wine. People were confused at first, but then Georg held several wine glass tastings where even novice wine tasters noticed the difference between the different glass shapes. He was later awarded Decanter Man of the Year for his contribution to the wine world. So, what shapes are right for which wines? Let's take a look.

- **Red Wines – Fuller, Rounder Glasses with Larger Openings**

The reason for this has to do with surface area. Red wines need a larger surface area to soften and breathe. The wider openings and fuller, rounder glasses allow more air to enter the glass and interact with the wine. When that happens, both evaporation and oxidation take place, and those processes change the chemistry of the wine. For red wines, those changes improve their quality. Since red wines are more prone to contain volatile compounds, the larger surface area of the glass allows those volatile compounds to dissipate quickly. Additionally, sulfites in wine disperse when it is given time to breathe. The oxidation lets the flavors and aromas shine through. This is particularly true for wine that has been stored for a long period of time in a cellar. Since the wine has been 'closed' for some time, the larger glass allows the compounds to disperse and the wine can open up.

- **Taller Glasses for Some Reds**

Most red wines benefit from larger glasses, but some types of reds also benefit from a taller height of the glass. A tall wine glass with a broad bowl is often referred to as a Bordeaux glass, and it is designed for full-bodied reds like Cabernet Sauvignon and Syrah. This type of glass directs the wine to the back of the mouth. The shorter glasses with large bowls are called Burgundy glasses, and they direct delicate wines like Pinot Noir to the tip of the tongue.

- **Smaller Bowls for White Wines**

White wines do not require as large a bowl as reds in order to release their aroma and flavor. Their glass should be more U-shaped and upright than that of a red wine. The U-shape allows the aroma to be released. Additionally, the smaller bowl helps retain a cooler temperature than the larger bowls. Youthful white wines, however, will benefit from a slightly larger opening so that they are directed to the tip and sides of the tongue. More mature whites are better served in straighter, taller glasses to direct the wine to the back and sides of the tongue. That allows you to taste the bolder, buttery, and oaky flavors.

- **A Slightly Flared Rim and Shorter Tapered Bowls for Rosés**

WHILE ROSÉS CAN BE SERVED IN WHITE WINE GLASSES, there are glasses specifically made for the fruity, slightly sweeter flavor characters of a rosé. They have shorter, slightly tapered bowls and a flared rim. This directs the wine to the tip of the tongue.

- **Tall and Narrow for Champagne**

Certain champagnes like Prosecco and Cava have lighter flavors that are well-suited to a tall, narrow glass. These types of glasses are often called flutes, and they capture the carbon dioxide in sparkling wines, which keeps the bubbles in the bubbly.

Some champagnes, however, are more suited to a wider, white wine-style glass, particularly those that are more complex. Just as with a still wine, the complex flavor compounds require a greater surface area to breathe.

Pouring the Wine

A bottle of wine contains a little over 25 ounces which makes it portioned for five services that are 5 ounces (150 ml) each. Many US restaurants will pour a more generous 6 ounce (180 ml) serving, which is nice when you're paying by the glass. Most wine glasses can hold much more – approximately 17 to 25 ounces, but remember the space is designed to hold the aromas, so you don't want to overfill your glass.

Now, you know about the art of serving wine. The next time you've got friends and family over for a good bottle, they'll be impressed with your new knowledge, and they'll appreciate it when they taste the wine!

CHAPTER SUMMARY

In this chapter, we've discussed the art of serving wine. Specifically, we've covered the following topics:

- Temperatures for serving;
- Cutting the foil;
- Proper use of the corkscrew and inspecting the cork;

- Decanting, aerating, and filtering wine;
- Use of the properly shaped glass;
- Pouring a standard glass of wine.

In the next chapter, you will learn more about the language of wine tasting.

CHAPTER NINE: CONVERSATIONS IN WINE – THE LANGUAGE OF WINE TASTING

I n Chapter Three, we covered numerous terms used to describe the character of the grape and wine, but there are many other vocabulary terms in the language of wine tasting that you should be aware of, since many, if not all, affect the taste of your wine. We'll take these terms alphabetically as we go along. As with any new vocabulary terms, a glass of wine is in order to help you remember them!

A IS FOR AMARONE

But, it's not first on our list.

Alsace: This refers to a wine region in France that is renowned for dry and sweet wines that are made from Riesling, Gewurztraminer, Pinot Blanc, Pinot Gris, and other grape varieties.

Amarone: It's second on our list. This refers to a succulent, higher-alcohol red wine that comes from the Veneto region in northern Italy. It's made primarily from Corvina grapes that are dried on racks before they are pressed.

AOC: This abbreviation stands for Appellation d'Origine Controlee. It is a French term that means the region is registered and properly denominated by the government.

AVA: This stands for American Viticultural Area, and it means a wine region has been named and approved by the Bureau of Alcohol, Tobacco, and Firearms.

B IS FOR BEAUJOLAIS

Bacchus: This is the Roman god of Wine. He was known as Dionysus in ancient Greece. The term also refers to a hybrid white grape from Germany.

Barrel Fermented: This refers to the process by which wine – usually white wine – is fermented in oak barrels as opposed to other tanks like those made of stainless steel. Barrel fermentation produces a richer, creamier, oakier style of wine.

Barrique: This the French word for 'barrel,' and generally, they are referring to a barrel of 225 liters.

Beaujolais: This is the juicy, flavorful red wine made with Gamay grapes and grown in the region of the same name.

Beaujolais Nouveau: This is the first Beaujolais of the harvest season. It is released annually on the third Thursday in November.

Blanc de Blancs: This is the name for Champagne that is made entirely from Chardonnay grapes.

Blanc de Noirs: This is the name for Champagne that is made completely from red grapes, either Pinot Noir, Pinot Meunier, or both.

Blend: This is the process by which two or more grape varieties are separately fermented, but then combined to produce such wines as Cotes du Rhone and the red and white Bordeaux.

Blush: This refers to wines made from red grapes, but which appear pink or salmon in color due to the fact that the grape skins were removed from the fermenting juice before the color was imparted. The more common term is rosé.

Bodega: This is the Spanish word for winery. It literally translates as the "room where barrels are stored."

Bordeaux: This is the city on the Garonne River in south-western France. It is a large winemaking region that includes more than a dozen subregions. The area produces red wines made mostly from Cabernet Sauvignon, Merlot, and Cabernet, and white wines made from Sauvignon Blanc and Semillon.

Botrytis cinerea: This is a beneficial mold that makes grapes shrivel as it also causes the sugars to concentrate. That results in a sweet, unctuous wine. Examples include Sauternes, Tokay, and the German Beerenauslese, which is a late harvest wine.

Breathe: This refers to the process of introducing air into the wine in order to open it up.

Brix: This is a scale used to measure the level of sugar in grapes prior to fermentation. To find the wine's future alcohol level, you multiply the brix by 0.55.

Brut: A French term that describes the driest Champagnes.

Burgundy: This is a prominent region in France that runs from Chablis in the north to Lyons in the south. The region is known for using the Pinot Noir grape to produce a red Burgundy and the Chardonnay grape is used for their white wines.

C IS FOR CHABLIS

Cap: This refers to grape solids such as pits, skins, and stems that will rise to the top of the tank during fermentation. It is the cap that gives red wines their color, tannins, and weight.

Chablis: This is both a wine region and a town east of Paris. It is known for a steely, minerally Chardonnay.

Chaptalization: This the process of adding sugar to grapes that are fermenting in order to increase their alcohol level.

Chateau: This is the French word for 'castle,' which refers to an estate that has its own vineyards.

Claret: This is the English name for a red Bordeaux.

Clos: This is pronounced, 'Cloh,' and it is the French word that was once used for vineyards surrounded by walls.

Cooperative: This is a winery that is owned jointly by multiple grape growers.

Crianza: This is a Spanish word for red wines aged in oak barrels for at least one year.

Cru: This is a French word for ranking a wine in inherent quality – for example, cru bourgeois, cru classe, premier cru, and grand cru.

D IS FOR DOURO

Denominación de Origen: This is the Spanish term for 'appellation of origin,' similar to the French AOC or the Italian DOC.

Denominazione di Origine Controllata: This is the Italian word for 'appellation of origin," and like the Spanish and French terms, it refers to wine regions that are strictly controlled by the government.

Disgorge: This is the process whereby the final sediments are removed from sparkling wines prior to adding the dosage (see below).

Dosage: This is the sweetened spirit that is added to the end of the process of making Champagne and other sparkling wines. It will determine whether it is a brut, extra dry, dry or semi-sweet sparkling wine.

Douro: This refers to the wine region and river in Portugal that is famous for producing Port wines.

E IS FOR ENJOY!

Enology: This is the word for the science of wine production. An enologist is a professional winemaker, and you and I are enophiles – people who enjoy wine.

F IS FOR FORTIFIED WINE

Fermentation: This is the process in which sugar is transformed into alcohol. It involves the chemical interaction between the grape juice and its natural yeast to produce wine.

Filtration: This refers to clarifying the wine prior to bottling.

Fining: This is part of that clarification process where certain elements, like egg whites, are added to the wine to capture the particulates prior to filtration.

Fortified Wine: This refers to wines that have brandy added during the fermentation process. Because of the addition of alcohol, sugars and sweetness are high in a fortified wine.

G IS FOR GAMAY

Gamay: This is a very popular grape in the Beaujolais region of France.

Graft: This refers to a technique used by vineyards for attaching the bud-producing part of a grapevine to an existing root.

Gran Reserva: This is the Spanish term for those wines which are aged in wood and bottles for at least five years before they are released for sale.

Grand Cru: See Cru – this French phrase means 'great growth,' and refers to the very best vineyards.

Grenache: This is a hearty, productive, and popular red grape in southern France and Spain. In the latter, it is called Garnacha.

Grüner Veltliner: This is a white grape that is popular in Austria. It makes lean, fruity, and racy wines.

H IS FOR HYBRID

Haut: This French word means 'high.' and it is used to describe wine quality as well as altitude.

Hectare: This is a measure of land equal to 10,000 square meters or 2.47 acres.

Hectoliter: This is a metric measurement that equals 100 liters or 26.4 gallons.

Hollow: This term describes wine that is lacking in depth or body.

Hybrid: This is the genetic crossing of two or more grape types. A few common hybrids are Muller-Thurgau and Bacchus.

I IS FOR ICE WINE

Ice Wine: This is also commonly known by the German term eiswein. It is a wine made from frozen grapes, and Germany, Austria, and Canada are the leading producers.

J IS FOR JEROBOAM

Jeroboam: This refers to an oversized bottle that is equal to six regular 750 ml bottles.

K IS FOR KABINETT

Kabinett: This is the German word for high-quality wines, typically the driest of Rieslings.

Kosher: This refers to wine that is made in accordance with strict Jewish rules under rabbinical supervision.

L IS FOR LABRUSCA

Labrusca: This refers to those grape types that are native to North America, including Concord and Catawba.

Late Harvest: This describes dessert wines that are made from grapes left for an extended period of time on the vine, often until Botrytis has set in.

Lees: This is the heavy sediment that is left in the barrel after the fermentation process. It is a combination of spent yeast, cells, and grape solids.

Loire: This is a river in central France that runs through the wine region of the same name. The region is renowned for Chenin Blanc, Sauvignon Blanc, and Cabernet Franc.

M IS FOR MEDOC

Maceration: This refers to a process of letting grape juice and skins ferment together, which imparts color, tannins, and aromas to the wine.

Maderized: This word comes from the word for the island Madeira, but it means oxidation in a hot environment, as happens on Madeira.

Magnum: This refers to a bottle that is equal to two regular 750 ml bottles.

Medoc: This is a wine region of Bordeaux located on the west bank of the Gironde Estuary. It is known for great red wines, such as Margaux, St.-Estephe, and Pauillac.

Must: This refers to the crushed grapes that are either about to go through or already going through fermentation.

N IS FOR NEGOCIANT

Negociant: This is the French term for someone or a company that buys wines from others and then labels it under their own name. It comes from the French word for 'shipper.'

O IS FOR ORGANIC

Organic: This means the grapes were grown without using chemical-based fertilizers, pesticides, or herbicides.

Oxidized: This refers to wine that is not fresh anymore because it was exposed to too much air.

P IS FOR PREMIER CRU

pH: This refers to the wine's acidity level. It is expressed by how much hydrogen it contains.

Phylloxera: This is a voracious little vine louse that has destroyed many vineyards in Europe and California.

Plonk: This term is used to describe cheap, poor-tasting wine.

Pomace: This is the mass of skins, pits, and stems that remain after the fermentation process. They are used to make grappa in Italy and marc in France.

Premier Cru: This is French for 'first growth,' and it refers to a high-quality vineyard, but it is not the highest quality. For those, the term is 'Grand Cru.'

Press: This is the process of extracting grape juice prior to fermentation using a machine.

Primeur (en): This is the French word for wine that is sold while it is still in the barrels. It is known as 'futures' in countries where English is spoken.

R IS FOR RESERVA

Racking: This is the word for the process of moving wine from barrel to barrel, and thereby, leaving sediment behind.

Reserva: This is the Spanish word for red wine that has been in barrels and bottles for at least three years prior to release.

Reserve: This American term indicates a higher quality of wine, but it has no legal meaning.

Riddling: This is the process of rotating Champagne bottles for the purpose of shifting the sediment toward the cork.

S is for Sancerre

Sancerre: This is the region in the Loire Valley that is known mostly for wines made from Sauvignon Blanc.

Silky: This refers to wines made with a smooth feel in the mouth.

Solera: This is the Spanish system of blending wines of different ages. They do it to create a harmonious end product; a stack of barrels that holds wines of various ages.

Sommelier: This refers to a wine steward, but it is generally someone with a great amount of wine knowledge, and who usually holds a diploma of sorts in wine studies.

Split: This is a quarter bottle of wine – that means it is a single serving bottle equal to 175 milliliters.

Steely: This refers to describe a very crisp, acidic wine that has not been aged in barrels.

Stemmy: This term describes harsh, green characters in wine.

Super Tuscan: This is a red wine from Tuscany that is not made according to the Italian DOC rules; rather, it is blended, of superior quality, and it contains Cabernet Sauvignon and/or Merlot.

T IS FOR TEMPRANILLO

Table Wine: This phrase refers to wines between 10 and 14 percent alcohol. In Europe, a table wine is one that is made outside of a regulated region or using methods not approved by the government.

Tempranillo: This refers to the most popular red grape in Spain. It is commonly used in Rioja and Ribera del Duero.

Trocken: This is the German word for 'dry.'

V IS FOR VIN SANTO

Vin Santo: This is a sweet wine made in Tuscany from late-harvest Trebbiano and Malvasia grapes.

Vintage: This is the term for a particular year in the wine business. It refers to a specific harvest.

Viticulture: This is the word that means the science and business of growing wine grapes.

Y IS FOR YEAST? YES, YEAST!

Yeast: These lovely little organisms – in the wine business anyway – are responsible for producing the enzymes that trigger the fermentation process. They can be natural or commercial, and are partly responsible for the distinctive wine characters.

Yield: This refers to the amount of grapes harvested in a particular year.

Z IS FOR ZINFANDEL

Zinfandel: This is the popular grape used in California that is of disputed origin. Scientists say it is related to grapes from Croatia and southern Italy.

And,. there you have it! You're now all caught up on the common terminology in the wine business. Don't forget the terms for describing wine and grape characters in Chapter Three, but now you have a good grasp of the language of wine. But, it wouldn't be a vocabulary lesson if you didn't practice. So, your homework is to go to a wine tasting event and start talking about the characters, wine regions, grapes, and processes used to make your favorite varietals!

CHAPTER SUMMARY

In this chapter, we've discussed the language of wine. Specifically, we covered the following topics:

- The terms, phrases, and wine varieties that have not been described elsewhere in the book;
- The need to practice your new vocabulary by attending a wine tasting event.

In the next chapter, you will learn about the health benefits of wine consumption.

CHAPTER TEN: RED, WHITE, AND YOU – HEALTH BENEFITS OF WINE

S o frequently, our favorite things are bad for us, but not in this case. So, pour another glass of that healthy wine and let's talk about the health benefits of wine.

WHILE BOTH RED AND WHITE WINES IMPART SOME
health benefits because of the antioxidants they contain –
they are made from grapes, after all – red wine really comes
out the winner as the more healthy of the two. And, many
cultures seem to have been clued into that fact for a long
period of time. In fact, monks in Medieval monasteries
believed they lived longer in part because of their habit of
moderate wine consumption. And, more recently, scientific
studies have shown that to be true. A 2018 study found positive benefits associated with drinking red wine in moderation
with regard to the following (Seitz, 2020):

- cardiovascular disease;
- atherosclerosis;
- hypertension;
- some cancers;
- type 2 diabetes;
- neurological disorders;
- metabolic syndrome.

So, how was it helping? Well, it turns out that the skin of
grapes, particularly dark grapes, is a rich source of something
called resveratrol, a natural antioxidant that has anti-inflam-
matory and lipid-regulating effects. The benefits of antioxidants have been demonstrated for helping with many
diseases, including cancer and heart disease, and these are
contained in many healthy foods such as fruits, nuts, and
vegetables. And, that's what makes that tasty glass of Pinot
Noir healthy for you. But, let's look a little more closely at
what it might be doing to help with specific conditions.

Cardiovascular health: Several studies have shown positive links between drinking red wine in moderation and good
heart health. A review of studies in 2019 reported that red
wine consumption – in moderation, always in moderation, is

linked with a lower risk of coronary heart disease. That's a leading cause of disease and death in the United States. The authors who conducted the review noted that the red wine seemed to have protective effects for heart health. Now, there may be other factors in play here, and consuming too much alcohol does far more damage than good, but if you stay within the CDC guidelines for moderate drinking, red wine appears to impart some benefits for heart health. The CDC guidelines are one glass of wine per day for women and two glasses for men – those lucky devils (Seitz, 2020).

Gut health: Another study, conducted in 2018, reported that the polyphenols in red wine – and also those in grapes – help to improve the gut microbiota. That's a fancy word that means the microscopic organisms that live in your intestines and are a major part of good health. You want to keep them happy, and apparently, they like red wine. A separate study also noted that red wine contains compounds that also act like probiotics and boost healthy gut bacteria. Another plus is that the effects on the microbiome also help reduce the risk of heart disease (Seitz, 2020). It's a win-win – good from mouth to gut!

Type 2 diabetes: A study conducted in 2015 showed that a glass of red wine consumed with dinner modestly decreased cardiometabolic risk in people with type 2 diabetes. That refers to the possibility that you can build up plaque-like substances in your arteries that could block the artery and cause a heart attack. People with type 2 diabetes, often because of concurrent obesity, can be at more of a risk for that, but luckily red wine can help (Seitz, 2020).

Hypertension: The resveratrol in wine as well as compounds called procyanidins both act to keep blood vessels healthy and increase levels of HDL (that's the good kind) cholesterol. Those effects then reduce blood pressure (Seitz, 2020). And, who doesn't find a glass of wine relaxing?

Brain damage following a stroke: Another review of studies conducted in 2015 showed that resveratrol can help protect against brain damage following a stroke or other central nervous system injury. That's because of its positive effect on inflammation, oxidative stress, and cell death (Seitz, 2020).

Vision loss: Again, the resveratrol is the active ingredient here that may help prevent vision loss by reducing inflammation and oxidative stress. This can help prevent vision loss due to a number of conditions where those are common, such as glaucoma, cataracts, diabetic retinopathy, and macular degeneration (Seitz, 2020).

Cancer: Some of the research indicates that red wine consumption may help reduce the risk of certain cancers, though the National Cancer Institute is quick to say that alcohol consumption can cause certain cancers too. Still, a number of studies link moderate red wine consumption with better outcomes in cancer patients. Here are a few that research suggests red wine consumption could help:

- Breast cancer: Alcohol increases estrogen in the body, and that can encourage the growth of cancer cells. But, red wine – and to a lesser extent, white wine – contains substances called aromatase inhibitors (AIs), and these AIs may reduce estrogen levels and increase testosterone levels in women who are nearing menopause. For that reason, red wine – and wine in general – is less associated with an increased risk for breast cancer than other kinds of alcohol (Seitz, 2020).
- Lung cancer: Here again, the hero is resveratrol. It appears to have protective effects against cancer in both human and laboratory studies. It appears

that it prevents cell proliferation and tumor growth, which inhibits metastasis (Seitz, 2020).

- Prostate cancer: In a 2019 study, men who drank red wine had a slightly lower risk of lethal prostate cancer as the wine tended to slow the progression of the disease (Seitz, 2020).

Dementia: A 2018 report noted that researchers found an increased risk of dementia in people who didn't drink wine. This may be due to the neuroprotective effects of those polyphenols that help to reduce inflammation and promote healthy lipids (Seitz, 2020).

Depression: It appears red wine is not just good for your physical health, but your mental health as well. In a 2013 study on over 5,505 people, those who drank between 2 and 7 glasses of wine per week had lower levels of depression (Seitz, 2020). Most wine drinkers can tell you that.

Liver disease: While alcohol is a common cause of liver disease, a moderate consumption of red wine appears to promote good liver health by lowering fibrosis in those people who suffer from a non-alcohol related fatty liver disease. Again, this may be related to the antioxidants and reduction of oxidative stress (Seitz, 2020).

Longer life: Because the moderate consumption of red wine can reduce the risk of certain chronic diseases, it follows that it can help people to live longer. A 2000 study showed that men between the ages of 45 and 64 who drank about 5 drinks per day did have a longer life expectancy than either occasional or heavy drinkers (Seitz, 2020). Now, that may have been due to confounding factors like other healthy life-style habits, but still...you gotta wonder!

So, if you're wondering whether you should drink red or white wine, it looks like a good red wine will have better health benefits, but white wines also impart some benefits.

They just don't contain as much resveratrol as red wines. It's also true that non-alcoholic red wines would contain resveratrol as well. And, of course, all of the potential health benefits we've discussed come with the caveat that we're talking about consuming red wine **in moderation**. Just like with anything else, too much of a good thing can be a bad thing. So, don't overdo it, because excessive alcohol consumption causes far more deaths than the lives saved by moderate red wine consumption. And, excessive alcohol consumption puts you at risk for a number of problems including heart disease, stroke, liver damage, certain cancers, pancreatitis, and mental health problems. You can also kill yourself by drinking too much alcohol. The point is don't overdo it, but the point also is that if you drink red wine in moderation, it can have certain health benefits that could help you to live longer. That's something worth your glass of wine for!

CHAPTER SUMMARY

In this chapter, we've discussed the health benefits of moderate wine consumption. Specifically, we've covered the following topics:

- Red wine versus white wine – red wine has more helpful compounds for health;
- The main ingredient that helps fight off various disease conditions appears to be resveratrol;
- The various conditions that research has shown moderate red wine consumption may help, including heart disease, certain cancers, dementia, and much more.

In the next chapter, I'll have a few final thoughts.

FINAL WORDS

Wine consumption has a long and venerated history in human culture. It has been described as the nectar of the gods, and indeed, many cultures assign particular gods to its production. It has been used in religious rituals and other cultural rites throughout history. And, in our modern world, there's nothing better than relaxing with a fine glass of wine after a long, hard day at work. In fact, some research shows (Seitz, 2020) it may help lower your blood pressure and help you live longer.

If you're like many people, you may have often thought about learning more about that tasty elixir, and now you have a guide that you can use to describe your favorite variety as you talk like a pro about its distinctive characters and the production process. This book puts the terminology and information about some of the world's best wines right in your hand – or on your cell phone as the case may be.

Now, you know about how that grape gets turned into your favorite Chardonnay. You also know where the term Chardonnay comes from, what regions in the world make it, and the different processes used by vineyards to produce it. You also know how to serve that tasty treat when you have your friends over for your own wine tasting event. And, you'll no longer feel put off by the language used to describe wines when you visit a winery to sample new vintages. You also know what vintage means and how to properly read a wine label.

This book is now your own personal guide to the fascinating and tasty world of wine. You have at your fingertips something to refer to when you're sampling new varietals or just talking about the best wine-producing regions in the world. You're now familiar with the terms that refer to good quality wine and those that indicate a bad turn of events. What's more, you get to apply your new-found knowledge every time you buy another bottle of your favorite Bordeaux. You know what to look for on the label, where the wine was made, and from what type of grape. And, you know how to determine if the wine was made under strict government regulations so that you can trust the quality of the production process. You know there is such a thing as good yeast, and how the land the grapes are grown on contributes to the wine's distinctive flavor, something you know is called terroir.

This book has helped you to go from novice to pro, or maybe it has just helped you to enjoy more fully that next glass of your favorite Pinot Noir. Whether you wanted to just know more about wine or you're hoping to impress your friends and family, there's no doubt that you now have the information you need for either objective. They'll marvel at your next dinner party how well you paired the meal with that bottle of wine, and they'll be fascinated to hear what you've learned. And, you'll find your palate will develop and improve the more you savor your favorite wines instead of simply drinking them down. Everyone will get more enjoyment out of that next bottle thanks to your effort to educate yourself. That's right, pat yourself on the back, but even better...

Sit back, cut the foil below the rim of the bottle, set your corkscrew in just off-center so the worm will be centered as it penetrates the cork (but not all the way through), pop that cork, inspect it, decant the wine, pour it into a properly-shaped glass, swirl it to aerate the wine, get your nose in there, savor the aromas, take a sip, aspirate the wine, describe the characters in your notebook, and enjoy! Enjoy not only the taste of this magic elixir, but the fruits (pardon the pun) of your labor. You decided to take on the challenge of learning more about wine, and you have achieved your goal. Now, get out there and drink to your health!

SOURCES

Alech, A. (2017, August 8). 5 Classifications of Wine: Still Wine, Sparkling Wine, Fortified Wine, Brandy, Grappa & Vermouth. Retrieved June 3, 2020, from https://www.winefrog.com/5-classifications-of-wine-still-sparkling-fortified/2/2202

Bhatnagar, S. (2019, March 19). Red Wine Or White Wine: Which Is Better For Your Health? Retrieved June 3, 2020, from https://food.ndtv.com/food-drinks/red-wine-or-white-wine-which-is-better-for-your-health-1834678.

Burgess, L. (2016, August 21). The Crush Is The First Step In Turning Grapes Into Wine. Retrieved June 3, 2020, from https://vinepair.com/articles/the-crush-is-the-first-step-in-turning-grapes-into-wine/

California Wine Club. (n.d.). Wine Tasting Terms - Sound Like A Wine Pro With These Wine Words. Retrieved June 3, 2020, from https://www.cawineclub.com/wine-tasting-terms

Clemens, G. (2018, June 27). Wine categories and what they mean. Retrieved June 3, 2020, from https://eu.gosanangelo.com/story/life/columnists/gus-clemens/2018/06/27/wine-categories-and-what-they-mean/692309002/

Firpo, E. (2018, August 21). How to Train Your Wine Palate. Retrieved June 3, 2020, from https://www.winemag.com/2018/08/21/train-wine-palate/

Fuller, R. (2014, December 23). 'Let us adore and drink!' A brief history of wine and religion. Retrieved June 3, 2020, from https://theconversation.com/let-us-adore-and-drink-a-brief-history-of-wine-and-religion-35308

Hancock, E. (2018, April 25). Wine glasses to use for different types of wine, explained. Retrieved June 3, 2020, from https://www.thedrinksbusiness.com/2018/04/the-wine-glasses-to-use-for-different-types-of-wine-explained/7/

Karlsson, P. (2019, April 14). World wine production reaches record level in 2018, consumption is stable | BKWine Magazine |. Retrieved June 3, 2020, from https://www.bkwine.com/features/more/world-wine-production-reaches-record-level-2018-consumption-stable/

Kettmann, M. (2017, May 4). 14 Rules for Winery Tasting Room Etiquette | Do's and Don'ts for a Successful Winery Trip. Retrieved June 3, 2020, from https://www.winemag.com/2015/08/13/14-rules-for-visiting-a-tasting-room/

Leon, J. (2016, August 3). The Art of Serving Wine.

Retrieved June 3, 2020, from
https://www.jeanleon.com/en/the-art-of-serving-wine/

LucAris. (2018, August 23). 5 Basic Types of Wine.
Retrieved June 3, 2020, from
https://www.lucariscrystal.com/5-basic-types-of-wine/

MarketView Liquor. (2018, July 30). How to Choose a
Good Wine. Retrieved June 3, 2020, from
https://www.marketviewliquor.com/blog/2018/08/how-to-
choose-a-good-wine/

Monte Creek Ranch. (2019, February 19). What you need to
know about winter pruning. Retrieved June 3, 2020, from
https://www.montecreekranch.com/what-you-need-to-know-
about-winter-pruning/

More Than Organic. (n.d.). Fermentation and wine making.
Retrieved June 3, 2020, from
https://www.morethanorganic.com/fermentation

Napa Valley Vintners. (2017, July 7). From Vine to Wine:
The Life Cycle of a Grape. Retrieved June 3, 2020, from
https://harvestnapa.com/all-about-harvest/from-vine-to-
wine-the-life-cycle-of-a-grape/

Phillips, R. (2011, October 20). Ancient Wine: Then and
Now. Retrieved June 3, 2020, from
https://www.guildsomm.com/public_content/features/article
s/b/rod_phillips/posts/ancient-wine-then-and-now

Slinkard, S. (2019a, August 7). Types of Fortified Wines You
Might Enjoy Before or After Dinner. Retrieved June 3, 2020,

from https://www.thespruceeats.com/what-is-a-fortified-wine-3510908

Slinkard, S. (2019b, November 7). Best of the Bubbles - Discover Four Types of Sparkling Wine. Retrieved June 3, 2020, from https://www.thespruceeats.com/types-of-sparkling-wine-3895624

Smith, A. (2020, April 21). Red wine: Benefits and risks. Retrieved June 3, 2020, from https://www.medicalnewstoday.com/articles/265635

Sullivan, S. (2018, November 13). Should You Smell the Cork When Opening Wine? Always. Retrieved June 3, 2020, from https://www.winemag.com/2018/11/12/smelling-wine-cork-when-open-wine/

Teeter, A. (2016a, June 3). Explaining Old World Wines Versus New World Wines [MAP]. Retrieved June 3, 2020, from https://vinepair.com/wine-blog/understanding-difference-old-new-world-wines/

Teeter, A. (2016b, June 3). Explaining Old World Wines Versus New World Wines [MAP]. Retrieved June 3, 2020, from https://vinepair.com/wine-blog/understanding-difference-old-new-world-wines/

Wikipedia contributors. (2020a, January 6). Wine in China - Wikipedia. Retrieved June 3, 2020, from https://en.wikipedia.org/wiki/Wine_in_China#Wine-producing_regions

Wikipedia contributors. (2020b, March 19). Georgian wine -

Wikipedia. Retrieved June 3, 2020, from
https://en.wikipedia.org/wiki/Georgian_wine

Wikipedia contributors. (2020c, May 17). New World wine
- Wikipedia. Retrieved June 3, 2020, from
https://en.wikipedia.org/wiki/New_World_wine

Wikipedia contributors. (2020d, May 21). Wine - Wikipedia. Retrieved June 3, 2020, from
https://en.wikipedia.org/wiki/Wine

Wikipedia contributors. (2020e, May 27). Argentine wine -
Wikipedia. Retrieved June 3, 2020, from
https://en.wikipedia.org/wiki/
Argentine_wine#Grape_varieties_and_wines
Wikipedia contributors. (2020f, May 30). Phylloxera - Wikipedia. Retrieved June 3, 2020, from
https://en.wikipedia.org/wiki/Phylloxera

Wine Enthusiast. (2017, May 4). Wine Terms- Wine 101 A
Glossary of Wine Terminology & Wine Dictionary.
Retrieved June 3, 2020, from
https://www.winemag.com/glossary/

Wine Folly. (2019a, September 7). An Overview of Mexican
Wine Country. Retrieved June 3, 2020, from
https://winefolly.com/deep-dive/an-overview-of-mexican-
wine-country/

Wine Folly. (2019b, September 10). 5 Types of Dessert
Wine. Retrieved June 3, 2020, from
https://winefolly.com/deep-dive/types-dessert-wine/

Wine Folly. (2019c, September 10). 7 Basics to Serving Wine

and Glassware. Retrieved June 3, 2020, from https://winefolly.com/tips/basics-serving-wine-glassware/

Wine Folly. (2020, May 16). Discover the Lifecycle of a Wine Grapevine. Retrieved June 3, 2020, from https://winefolly.com/deep-dive/lifecycle-of-a-wine-grapevine/

Wine For Rookies, Inc. (n.d.-a). New World Wine. Retrieved June 3, 2020, from http://www.wineforrookies.com/wine-regions/new-world-wine

Wine For Rookies, Inc. (n.d.-b). Old World Wine. Retrieved June 3, 2020, from http://www.wineforrookies.com/wine-regions/old-world-wine

Wine Frog. (2016, November 27). What is Character (in Wine)? - Definition from WineFrog. Retrieved June 3, 2020, from https://www.winefrog.com/definition/4/wine-character

Wine to Cellar. (n.d.). grape varieties, types of grapes, flavour characteristics of grapes, wine grapes. Retrieved June 3, 2020, from https://www.click-on-wine.com/grape-varieties-for-wine.html

Winerist. (n.d.). Magazine - Wine Tasting Etiquette: The Dos and Don'ts | Winerist. Retrieved June 3, 2020, from https://www.winerist.com/magazine/wine/the-dos-and-donts-of-wine-tasting

Wines.com. (n.d.). Wine Varietals A-Z ‹ Wines.com. Retrieved June 3, 2020, from https://www.wines.com/wine-varietals/

Printed in Great Britain
by Amazon